Assessing Bank Reform

Assessing Bank Reform: FDICIA One Year Later

Edited by

GEORGE G. KAUFMAN AND ROBERT E. LITAN

Erratum

The table on page 28 belongs on page 74;
the table on page 74 belongs on page 28.

THE BROOKINGS INSTITUTION / Washington, D.C.

Copyright 1993

THE BROOKINGS INSTITUTION

1775 Massachusetts Avenue, N.W., Washington, D.C. 20036

Library of Congress Cataloging-in-Publication data:

Assessing Bank Reform: FDICIA One Year Later / [edited by]
George G. Kaufman and Robert E. Litan.
    p. cm.
    Includes bibliographical references.
    ISBN 0–8157-4874–4 : $29.95.—ISBN 0–8157-4873–6 (pbk.) :
$11.95
    1. Banks and banking—Government policy—United States—
Congresses.   2. Deposit insurance—United States—Congresses.
3. Deposit insurance—Law and legislation—United States—Congresses.   4. United States. Federal Deposit Insurance Corporation
Improvement Act of 1991—Congresses.   5. Federal Deposit Insurance Corporation—Congresses.   I. Kaufman, George G.
HG2491.F35   1993
332.1'0973—dc20   93–11151
                                                     CIP

9 8 7 6 5 4 3 2 1

The paper used in this publication meets the minimum requirements of the American National Standard for Information Sci-
ences—Permanence of paper for Printed Library Materials, ANSI
Z39.48–1984

Foreword

In December 1991, President Bush signed into law perhaps the most far-reaching reform of banking legislation since the Depression—the Federal Deposit Insurance Corporation Improvement Act of 1991 (FDICIA). The act was meant to be a direct response to the massive losses from the savings and loan debacle and the growing costs of bank failures.

FDICIA is sweeping and complex. Its most important—and perhaps most misunderstood—feature is to provide greater discipline against excessive risk-taking by banks through the mandating of early regulatory intervention, prompt failure resolution, and risk-based deposit insurance premiums. The act also requires a large number of new rules to implement these and other provisions. The new rules, in turn, have generated considerable controversy within the banking industry.

To mark the first anniversary of FDICIA, Brookings sponsored a one-day symposium on December 16, 1992, to assess the act's impact. The symposium was held shortly after the presidential election and thus also afforded a timely opportunity to discuss the potential changes in banking regulation that a Clinton administration was expected to bring. Speakers at the symposium included a broad range of experts from academia, industry, and the policymaking community. This volume contains the papers and written remarks of the formal discussants at the symposium. The concluding section of the volume contains a summary of the remarks and comments of the approximately 150 attendees. The papers have been edited for publication, but the book has not been subjected to the Institution's normal review and verification procedures.

The editors of this volume, who also presented papers at the symposium, are George G. Kaufman, professor of finance at Loyola University of Chicago, and Robert E. Litan, a senior fellow in the Brookings Economic Studies program and director of the Institution's Center for Law, Economics, and Politics. The editors are grateful for the research assistance of Kirsten Wallenstein, the secretarial assistance of Anita Whitlock, and the editing of Patricia Dewey.

Partial funding for this project was provided by Chicago Clearing House Association.

The views expressed here are those of the authors and editors and should not be attributed to their organizations or to the trustees, officers, or other staff members of the Brookings Institution.

Bruce K. MacLaury
President

June 1993
Washington, D.C.

Contents

GEORGE G. KAUFMAN AND ROBERT E. LITAN

Introduction and Summary

The last decade has been both traumatic and revolutionary for the U.S. banking industry. Accustomed to steady profits and few failures for the thirty-five years after World War II, the industry and the firms within it have since been buffeted by various market forces that have produced the largest number of bank failures—more than 1,000—and the worst loan losses since the Great Depression of the 1930s. In the process, in the 1980s, the average U.S. bank earned less for its shareholders, approximately 10 percent on their equity, than the typical manufacturing enterprise, which posted a 13 percent rate of return.

In late 1990 and early 1991—a period marking the bottom of the most recent recession—the outlook for the banking industry, and even for the federal insurance fund that backs most of its deposits, was especially bleak. Several independent analysts, congressional watchdog agencies, and the federal government itself (through the Office of Management and Budget) warned that the large number and size of bank failures would exhaust the resources of the Federal Deposit Insurance Corporation (FDIC) to resolve bank failures and pay off their depositors, as had occurred earlier for the Federal Savings and Loan Insurance Corporation (FSLIC) in the savings and loan debacle. At the same time, the stock market had severely discounted the share prices of most large banks well below their book value. Pessimism, if not alarm, about the state of the banking industry was the order of the day.

It was in this environment that in early 1991 the Senate and House Banking Committees each introduced bills calling for major deposit insurance reform. The Bush administration proposed similar reform, along with the most sweeping revision of the nation's banking laws since the 1930s and added borrowing authority for the FDIC. Included among the reform proposals were measures to strengthen bank capital standards and regulators' enforcement of them, to reduce the risk-taking incentives inherent in deposit insurance, to allow banks and their holding companies to operate in all states, to permit well-

1

capitalized bank holding companies to engage in a wide range of financial services then off limits (most important, the selling and underwriting of insurance and securities), and to permit nonfinancial firms to own bank holding companies.

Many of the proposals followed, and built on, the new internationally agreed upon system of bank capital standards, the so-called Basle Agreement, reached by bank regulators from the United States, Japan, and the major Western European countries. Unlike earlier capital standards, which required banks to back only their on-balance sheet assets with a certain percentage of capital, the Basle standards required capital backing of a variety of off-balance sheet guarantees and arrangements as well. In addition, the Basle standards introduced a new risk-weighting procedure that required assets considered by regulators to be riskier, such as most loans, to have more capital supporting them than such less risky assets as government securities. The Basle rules became partially effective in 1991 and fully effective in 1993.

Congress ultimately enacted only a portion of the ambitious plans—the new capital-based system of early regulatory intervention to reduce the cost of failures to the FDIC, together with $30 billion in borrowing authority for the FDIC—while adding a variety of additional provisions ostensibly designed to protect consumers and to better ensure the safety and soundness of banks. Yet even in its stripped-down form, the final legislation—the Federal Deposit Insurance Corporation Improvement Act (FDICIA)—still stands as one of the most important, and controversial, pieces of banking legislation of the last fifty years. It is for this reason that the Brookings Institution, in conjunction with the Chicago Clearing House Association, sponsored a conference in December 1992 to mark the first anniversary of FDICIA and to assess its impact.

This volume contains the papers presented at the conference and a summary of the discussion of the more than 150 participants who attended it. In this introductory chapter we provide some context for the discussion and then briefly present some highlights of the papers.

Ironically, the condition of and concerns about the U.S. banking industry in late 1992, one year after FDICIA, were very different from those present at the time FDICIA was being debated and constructed in Congress. During 1992 industrywide bank profits soared to a record of more than $32 billion. To be sure, at year-end 1992 more than 800 of the nation's 12,000 banks were classified by regulators as problem banks, posing an unusual risk of failure. These banks held about $460 billion of the $3.5 trillion in assets of the banking system. Nevertheless, both the number of problem banks and the assets they held had begun to decline from earlier peak levels. Also, the stock prices of many banks, especially the nation's largest, had rebounded smartly from lows of two years earlier.

Meanwhile, the focus in the banking industry had changed markedly from December 1991, when the dominant political objective was to stem the number and cost of bank failures, to December 1992, when concerns centered on the business loans the banking industry was not making. In fact, all three presidential candidates in 1992 attacked either the banking industry or the regulators overseeing it, or both, for causing a "credit crunch"—denying loans to creditworthy borrowers and thereby contributing to the sluggishness of the economic recovery from the 1990–91 recession, the slowest of the postwar period. Many bankers not only agreed with the criticism of the regulators but argued that much of the blame rested with the tougher capital standards and enforcement policy mandated by FDICIA.

However, it is precisely those policies within the 1991 banking legislation that continue to be strongly supported by key congressional leaders, many healthy banks, key federal banking regulators, and many members of the academic community. These proponents argue that without tough rules requiring bank shareholders to have their own funds at risk, not just federally guaranteed deposits, bankers will not be able to absorb likely loan losses and will be tempted to take the "heads I win, tails the government loses" bets that characterized the thrift crisis of the 1980s.

The conference brought together people representing all these viewpoints, including academic scholars, current and former policymakers, and private sector experts, to consider and debate the wisdom of FDICIA and of future banking policy. The papers presented were discussed in four sessions: the intellectual and political history of the act, implementation of the act, responses of regulators and banks to the act, and the direction banking regulatory and legislative policy should next take. In addition, two leading bank policymakers—Representative Jim Leach (Republican of Iowa), the ranking minority member of the House Banking Committee, and David W. Mullins, vice-chairman of the Federal Reserve Board—presented keynote talks and addressed many of the issues that were separately examined in each of the four sessions. It is the purpose of this volume, as it was of the conference, to present the background that resulted in FDICIA's enactment, to help frame the current debate regarding its provisions, and perhaps to help resolve some of its more contentious issues.

FDICIA: WHERE DID IT COME FROM AND HOW DID IT HAPPEN?

FDICIA is a complicated, multipart piece of legislation. Much of the act was designed both to curb the incentives that deposit insurance gives to weakly capitalized insured banks to take excessive risks and to limit the cost of failures to the FDIC. Thus the act dealt with the most pressing public policy issue of its day. But, as already noted, the act also helps to recapitalize the FDIC, tightens the supervision of domestic offices of foreign banks, and contains a series of other regulatory provisions designed to better protect consumers and rein in bank managers and directors. To George Kaufman and George Benston, who opened the conference, the deposit insurance reform provisions were by far the most important parts of the act, especially the new system of mandated structured early intervention and resolution (SEIR) and the requirement that the FDIC vary its deposit insurance assessments by the risk of the institution insured.

As outlined in FDICIA, SEIR means that insured depository institutions should be required to back their assets with at least a minimum amount of capital, and if capital falls below that level, regulators are required to progressively tighten their regulation of the institutions, by, among other things, limiting their growth, payments of dividends and salaries, and other aspects of bank operations. If capital falls too low, but before it is fully depleted and turns negative, regulators are required to take control of the institution and to "resolve" it, either by merging it with a healthy partner, or liquidating it and paying off the insured deposits. If the net proceeds from a merger or liquidation are positive, they are turned over to the former shareholders. But if they are negative—that is, if the FDIC absorbs some loss—then at least that loss is lessened because the regulators took action at an "early stage." Ideally, of course, if SEIR works properly, banks would be deterred from failing, but in the event that some do fail, the insurer loses nothing, and deposit insurance is rendered redundant.

Kaufman and Benston show that the essential features in SEIR and risk-based insurance premiums were outlined in a series of academic publications spanning the decade before FDICIA's proposal and enactment. At the same time, however, he explains that both features of FDICIA are somewhat weaker than originally proposed. Although the FDIC has introduced a risk-based deposit insurance premium structure, the spread between the highest and lowest rates charged in the first year is only 8 basis points (0.08 percent) of deposits, considerably narrower than the relative risks of the institutions in these risk categories. Meanwhile, the SEIR system created by FDICIA departs from the original SEIR proposals in several respects: the statutory system contains fewer mandatory sanctions, is based on historical cost accounting rather than on market or current value accounting, and still permits federal regulators (although under narrower circumstances) to insure all deposits of large banks labeled as "too big to fail." In addition, the authors point out that because regulators retain discretion in valuing the loan portfolios of the institutions they supervise, they can choose, if they wish, not to delay or even to implement the SEIR provisions.

Nevertheless, Kaufman and Benston argue that, compared with the unstructured and loosely enforced capital standards that preceded it, FDICIA represents a major advance in bank regulation and deposit insurance reform. If faithfully followed, the SEIR provisions should reduce future deposit insurance losses and thus the probability of banks being a burden on taxpayers, and make it easier for policymakers to broaden the product and geographic powers of banks.

Robert Glauber, the under secretary of Treasury in the Bush administration who guided the drafting of that administration's ambitious financial modernization proposal, agrees with Kaufman and Benston that the capital-based system of early regulatory intervention in FDICIA was an important advance. However, he criticizes Congress for not going further by enacting the administration's proposals to broaden the permissible activities of bank holding companies and to authorize national interstate branching. Glauber, along with several other authors, also criticizes what he believes is an excessive degree of bank regulation embodied in FDICIA, including extensive "truth in savings" disclosures regarding deposit interest rates, new audit requirements, and provisions relating to bank management. In his paper, Glauber traces the legislative history of how Congress enacted only a portion of the administration's proposal, while adding a series of regulatory and other provisions.

Robert Glauber names several factors that made it difficult for the administration to win enactment of its proposal. For instance, the plan had to be considered by eight different legislative committees, each with different concerns. More important, the broader activity and geographic powers in the proposal were viewed—incorrectly in Glauber's view—as more of the type of deregulation that, in the growing conventional wisdom, contributed to the savings and loan crisis of the 1980s. Indeed, it was largely for this reason that the chairmen of both the Senate and House Banking Committees supported only a "narrow" bill, without the broader powers. The chairmen were strongly supported in this view by the securities and insurance industries, which opposed bank entry into their businesses, and by many smaller banks, which opposed nationwide banking. Taken together, all these obstacles proved to be more powerful than the two factors that the Bush Treasury Department had going for it: that the banking industry was in crisis and the FDIC required recapitalization, and that the Treasury proposal was broadly supported by all the federal banking regulators. Nevertheless, Glauber believes that the Treasury bill went further than many expected and that the groundwork has thus been laid for major structural reform to achieve long-run competitive viability for banking.

William Haraf, formerly a banking scholar at the American Enterprise Institute and now an official with Citicorp, agrees with Glauber that the original Treasury proposal was far preferable to the final legislation that Congress was able to enact. However, he also believes that while, in principle, the capital-based intervention provisions of FDICIA represent a worthy advance, in practice regulators have demanded that banks maintain capital-to-asset ratios 2 to 3 percentage points above the stated regulatory minimum levels. As a result, Haraf argues, many banks have contracted to an excessive degree, reducing their lending and thereby slowing the economic recovery. The additional paperwork and regulatory burden mandated by FDICIA, in Haraf's view, has only made matters worse.

Haraf believes that the recent trends following FDICIA's passage are likely to continue for some time in the future. Accordingly, securities markets and finance companies will continue to replace banks as sources of credit.

IMPLEMENTATION OF FDICIA

Students of the political process know that the implementation of legislative mandates by regulatory agencies can be as important, if not more important, than the underlying legislation itself. FDICIA is no exception to this pattern. Here, as elsewhere, academic scholars have a very different view from people in the private sector of how FDICIA is being implemented.

Karen Shaw, a leading consultant to banks and other financial institutions, opens the discussion of the implementation of FDICIA by focusing on three of its key provisions. She begins with the early or prompt corrective action provisions (SEIR), observing that the clear intent of Congress in enacting them was to *narrow* the discretion of regulators as to when to discipline weak depository institutions and in what manner. Whereas Kaufman and Benston fear regulators will still be able to frustrate the will of Congress in this respect by refraining from taking appropriate action, Shaw agrees with Haraf that regulators have since effectively set too stringent capital standards: not just a minimum of 8 percent of "risk-adjusted" assets, but, in practice, 10 percent of assets for banks to be considered "well capitalized." In addition, Shaw points out that Congress grafted a set of other trip wires onto the prompt corrective action framework, which the agencies have used to downgrade the ratings of certain institutions. She recommends that the regulators use the same trip wires—including the adequacy of an institution's management and its internal controls—also to *upgrade* institutions that rank high on these other, noncapital measures, a process she believes would provide positive incentives for depositories to reduce the riskiness of their operations.

With respect to FDICIA's provisions dealing with deposit insurance, Shaw observes, as do Kaufman and Benston, that the act does not slam the door shut on the "too big to fail" policy, which regulators have used in the past to protect all the deposits (but not the equity) of large banks, and not just the amounts under the insurance ceiling, currently $100,000 per account. She notes that the original Treasury proposal nevertheless would have strengthened depositor discipline of banks at least somewhat by curtailing the ability of depositors to gain insurance protection for multiple deposit accounts. Shaw believes the banking industry made a mistake by opposing this proposal, which ultimately was dropped from the bill.

Shaw then turns to the section of FDICIA requiring federal bank regulators to add a component for interest rate risk to the risk-based bank capital standards by June 1993. She reports that although the Basle committee continues to work on this question, within the United States the Federal Reserve has done the most work, issuing a proposal that, in her view, measures interest rate risk simplistically. Shaw points out that many large banks have much more sophisticated interest-rate-risk monitoring systems, which the adoption of the Fed's proposal would inappropriately rule out.

James Annable, the chief economist of the First National Bank of Chicago, is also critical of FDICIA and other recent trends in bank regulation that have been driving risk-taking out of the banking system. In the process, banks have been induced to charge more for their loans, a result that in turn has contributed to the increase in the share of bank asset portfolios invested in government securities rather than in business loans. Annable admits that FDICIA will improve the protection of the insurance fund, but in reducing risk-taking banks it is reducing the efficiency of financial intermediation performed by banks.

Annable concludes by observing that bank regulation will never be static because each regulatory change induces a private sector response. Most recently this game of cat and mouse is being played out through additional risk-taking by banks in the market for derivative securities and contracts, such as agreements to swap different interest payments (fixed for variable or vice versa) and off-balance sheet guarantees. It is no accident that regulators are now attempting to deal with this risk, but as with other areas of bank risk-taking, they will always be a step behind. The main reason for this, in Annable's view, is the presence of deposit insurance, which creates the perverse incentives for risk-taking that regulators try to prevent, but in the process only induces the banks whose deposits are insured to find new ways to take risk.

Kenneth Scott, a professor of law at Stanford and a former general counsel of the Federal Home Loan Bank Board, is the first of two academic scholars discussing the implementation of FDICIA who voice the opposite concern from that of the practitioners. Rather than being too restrictive, FDICIA still grants regulators too much discretion, which Scott (like Kaufman) fears that regulators will use by not stepping in to take the prompt disciplinary action that FDICIA theoretically mandates. He therefore urges that, at a minimum, regulators be required to document the reasons for their inaction in particular cases.

Scott also expresses concerns over how the regulatory agencies will implement FDICIA's direction to set "standards" required in Section 132, which are apart from the capital rules. The danger here is that any agency-specified rules could rigidly restrict bank management without improving bank safety. Scott recommends that instead of imposing rules directly on the banks, the agencies publish guidelines outlining the specific conditions in a bank that will normally trigger further agency investigation and possibly intervention.

Edward Kane, a professor of economics and banking at Boston College, reinforces the concerns expressed by Kaufman and Scott that regulators can defeat the purposes of FDICIA by delaying asset writedowns, and thus timely intervention, to prevent significant losses to the FDIC, and ultimately to taxpayers. In principle, FDICIA's prompt corrective action provisions are designed to prevent this outcome by imposing requirements on banks that are very similar to the covenants that banks impose on their own borrowers. But, in practice, Kane perceives that regulators are trying to preserve as much discretion as they can to avoid imposing the mandatory disciplinary measures that FDICIA requires. He accuses them, as well as the bank trade associations, of waging a nasty campaign against FDICIA using mischaracterization, exaggeration, and distortion.

TWO VIEWS FROM FEDERAL POLICYMAKERS

Two well-placed federal policymakers who played major roles in the construction and passage of FDICIA contributed to this volume.

The first, Representative Jim Leach, who is now the ranking Republican member of the House Banking Committee, strongly supported the capital-based early intervention provisions of the act. Leach begins by focusing on large banks, which, for much of the postwar period, were viewed as requiring less restrictive capital standards than smaller banks. The alleged reason for this difference in treatment, which was enshrined in regulatory practice, was that larger banks had more diversified loan portfolios and more sophisticated management. Leach observes that the experience of the 1980s demonstrated that, if anything, larger banks should have been required to meet higher, not lower, capital standards than their smaller competitors because it was the largest banks that displayed some of the worst management and the highest loan losses.

Leach notes that in helping to raise bank capital ratios, FDICIA did not have the draconian effects that some feared. Most large banks that needed to raise capital did so during 1992, a year in which the industry enjoyed record profits. It is from this strong capital position that banks are now able to help finance the recovery. However, Leach observes that the risk weights applied by the Basle risk-based capital standards to commercial and other loans (relative to the small or zero weights applied to government and agency securities) will inhibit banks from making some loans that they otherwise should be making and will thus contribute to the credit crunch.

Leach argues that, notwithstanding some claims that many insolvent banks remain open and should be closed, the FDIC is not facing anything close to the savings and loan disaster. However, he warned that the FDIC may be required to assume some of the costs of completing the S&L cleanup if Congress refuses to provide sufficient resources to finish the job. Indeed, the continued failure to complete the removal of insolvent S&Ls from the financial system will penalize healthy banks and thrifts that must continue to compete with institutions that do not belong in business.

David Mullins, the vice-chairman of the Federal Reserve Board and a former assistant secretary of the Treasury, who, along with Robert Glauber, helped draft the Bush administration's financial modernization package, agrees with Leach that the banking industry has made tremendous progress toward returning to financial health from its weakened condition at the time the package was proposed. At the same time, however, Mullins points to the significant volume of assets held by problem banks as evidence that government policymakers should not relax their vigilance.

Mullins agrees with those who have criticized FDICIA for imposing excessive regulatory burdens on banks without offsetting social benefits. He suggests that Congress imposed those costs as the price for raising the FDIC's borrowing authority to $30 billion, and, therefore, wonders if the banking industry might be able to reverse some of the more onerous regulatory requirements in FDICIA (other than the capital requirements) if it found a way to take the U.S. Treasury out of its current role as a backstop supporter for the FDIC.

Mullins disputes the claims that the risk weightings in the Basle capital standards have contributed to the decline in commercial lending by banks by inducing a corresponding increase in bank investments in government securities. Such claims stem from the fact that every $100 of bank loans must be backed by $8 in capital, whereas no capital is required to back a bank's investments in government securities. Mullins points out, however, that only a relative handful of all U.S. banks do not meet the so-called tier 1 capital ratio (the ratio of equity capital to risk-adjusted assets), and thus are even in a position to be influenced by the Basle risk weights in their investment policies. Moreover, Mullins cites the fact that credit unions, whose capital standards are not risk-weighted, have shifted their investment policies just as significantly toward government securities as have the banks. From this experience, Mullins finds it hard to blame the risk weights for inducing banks to tilt toward government securities investments rather than loans.

Nevertheless, Mullins concedes that banks have been discouraged from making some commercial loans in particular by excessively stringent loan documentation requirements and a trend, culminating in the passage of FDICIA, toward the use of rigid rules to evaluate loans. As a result, banks have moved away from making small business loans, which generally require judgment and which cannot be easily standardized. Mullins indicates that the Federal Reserve would work with the then-incoming Clinton administration to change the regulatory climate to induce banks to increase their small business lending without compromising bank safety.

RESPONSES TO FDICIA

Writing while on the staff of the Senate Banking Committee, Richard Carnell, newly appointed assistant secretary of the treasury and a principal drafter of FDICIA's deposit insurance reforms, strongly defends its prudential provisions, such as prompt corrective action, risk-based premiums, and least-cost resolution. In Carnell's view, these reforms ameliorate the perverse incentives created by the pre-FDICIA federal safety net for depository institutions to take excessive risk and for regulators to forbear or treat institutions as too big to fail. Although the reforms may entail some transitional pain, the end result will be highly constructive. The reforms will curtail forbearance and too-big-to-fail, increase market discipline, reduce losses to the deposit insurance fund, and diminish the subsidy weak institutions exact from healthy institutions through mispriced deposit insurance.

Carnell criticizes the "culture of ad hoc discretion"—a way of thinking that glorifies unfettered regulatory discretion and reflexively condemns FDICIA for limiting regulators' flexibility in dealing with troubled institutions. Statutory limits can, he maintains, actually improve supervision and regulation by counteracting perverse incentives, eliminating options that serve no useful purpose, and focusing the regulators' attention on how best to exercise their remaining discretion.

The other three papers in this part are critical of FDICIA and its aftermath. Jay Weintraub, a securities analyst specializing in the banking industry for Merrill Lynch, focuses largely on the mandates unrelated to the capital standards. In his view, these provisions will impose unnecessary audit fees, divert personnel time, and increase legal costs. Moreover, the added penalties for negligence by bank directors are likely to make it much more difficult for banks to attract qualified directors. As a result, these features of FDICIA, as well as the higher capital ratios, are likely to contribute to a continued erosion of the competitiveness of banks relative to other types of financial intermediaries and institutions. Looking to the future, Weintraub recommends that FDICIA be modified to reduce regulatory burden, to authorize nationwide banking, and to make greater use of subordinated debt in bank capital structures.

Richard Aspinwall, a vice president of Chase Manhattan Bank, also takes a dim view of FDICIA, reasoning that the "carrots" are not as strong as the "sticks." He notes that even without FDICIA banks have been pressured by an array of market and regulatory forces—lower costs of communication and information processing, inhibitions on diversification of bank activities, and steadily higher deposit insurance costs—that have caused banks to lose market share to other financial intermediaries. FDICIA will only accentuate these pressures.

Aspinwall notes that the act has already had several effects on banks. It has induced many to raise their capital-to-asset ratios, through combinations of reduced dividend payments, new equity issues, and asset shrinkage. In addition, banks have shifted away from intermediation, which uses capital intensively, to services, such as mutual fund sales, which are not intensive users of capital. But he notes that regulators have been slow in implementing many sections of the act.

As for the future, Aspinwall urges that policymakers recognize that in information-rich societies like the United States capital markets will continue to replace financial intermediaries as sources of finance. For this reason, new ways will have to be found to prevent intermediaries, such as banks, to pursue end-game strategies at the expense of the deposit insurance fund, and ultimately, of taxpayers. One way those expenses can be minimized is by liberalizing the operating powers of banks.

Finally, Anthony Downs of Brookings is critical of the way in which he believes regulators have overreacted to the very real banking problems they uncovered in Texas and later in New England. Although these reactions occurred well before FDICIA, the act has helped to codify this excessively restrictive regulatory environment, especially the hostile attitude toward bank lending for commercial real estate.

Downs recognizes that many, if not most, of the problems in commercial real estate predate FDICIA. Real estate construction has historically been one of the most cyclically sensitive sectors of the economy, and both builders and lenders went too far in sponsoring commercial construction projects during the 1980s. It was overbuilding that ultimately led to a real estate crisis, for which banks and financial intermediaries will continue to pay for many years to come.

Nevertheless, Downs believes that by forcing banks to suddenly and dramatically curtail their real estate lending, regulators deprived the market of liquidity, which has caused prices to be excessively depressed and has delayed the recovery in real estate markets. In turn, Downs argues that depressed real estate prices have resulted in excessive contraction in bank capital, which exacerbates an overall credit crunch. FDICIA and continuing congressional pressure on regulators contributes to this vicious cycle. The only silver lining that Downs sees in FDICIA is that by eventually leading to a better capitalized banking system, it may lay the foundation for banks at some future point to resume the more normal degree of risk-taking that is inherent in bank lending.

WHERE TO FROM HERE?

Lee Hoskins, former president of the Federal Reserve Bank of Cleveland and now president of the Huntington National Bank, a large regional bank in Ohio, suggests that FDICIA institutionalized a regulatory response to the moral hazard problem created by deposit insurance. However, the more efficient, but admittedly more politically difficult, way to address that problem would be to reduce the scope of deposit insurance itself. The key reason for this is that the regulatory structure mandated by FDICIA as a substitute for market discipline is inefficient and is proving to be highly burdensome for banks. This regulatory cost will continue to be large, if not increasing, as long as banks benefit from deposit insurance.

Hoskins outlines several strategies that banks can follow in a post-FDICIA environment. For example, they can urge policymakers to reduce regulatory burdens. Much can be done on this front by regulators themselves, but some steps require legislative action, such as the reversal of the truth-in-savings requirements in FDICIA, which Hoskins argues are especially burdensome. More fundamental reform of government deposit insurance, such as scaling it back or eliminating it altogether, clearly would require legislative approval. One way to develop political support for such an initiative, Hoskins points out, is to highlight the fact that deposit insurance disproportionately benefits wealthy or high-income individuals and families. Significantly, Hoskins cites results from a survey conducted by the Federal Reserve of Minneapolis indicating that more than 80 percent of the banks in the region would support a reduction in the amount of deposit insurance.

In the absence of fundamental reform, Hoskins suggests that banks will try to evade the costs of FDICIA and the regulatory environment by moving their activities off balance sheet. Ultimately, if regulatory burdens become excessive, Hoskins suggests that banks will ready themselves for sale, or get out of the "intermediation business" altogether.

Barbara Timmer, former chief counsel to the House Banking Committee who contributed to the drafting of FDICIA, believes that, notwithstanding the passage of the act, the banking system may continue to be plagued by a sizable failure problem in the future because banks will continue to be susceptible to declines in the value of their underlying collateral, principally real estate. FDICIA should nevertheless contain this risk by ensuring that when bank capital levels begin to fall, regulators will constrain the institutions from taking additional risk without restoring their capital to the required minimum.

Robert Litan concludes by distinguishing between two reform "agendas": the old one pursued by the last two administrations, which focused not just on correcting the weaknesses in the deposit insurance system but also on expanding geographic and product-line powers of banks and their holding companies, and a new agenda to be launched by the Clinton administration. Litan suggests that the outlook for the broader powers portion of the old agenda is uncertain, if not dim. However, like several others at the conference, he urges that the capital standards be revised not only to allow, but to mandate, larger banks to include as part of their required capital some subordinated (and thus uninsured) debt. This would ensure that larger institutions with the capacity to tap the capital markets would have to do so on a regular basis in order to expand, a result that would supplement regulatory discipline with a healthy dose of market discipline.

Litan observes that the Clinton administration is likely to focus the banking agenda not on previous administrations' topics of concern but on credit availability, especially for individuals and businesses in low-income regions and neighborhoods. The chief vehicle for accomplishing this objective outlined by the new president in his campaign is a proposal to create a network of community development banks (CDB). Litan notes that several important issues will have to be resolved in order for Clinton's CDB proposal to become a reality, including which types of institutions (such as banks, thrifts, and credit unions) will qualify as CDBs; whether, and to what extent, commercial banks will get credit toward their community investment requirements; and whether any or all of the final proposal will be submitted for congressional approval, or left to be implemented by regulators under existing law.

CONCLUDING ASSESSMENT

In sum, there was both consensus and division on FDICIA expressed at the conference. It was generally agreed, at least among those that commented on the issue, that those portions of FDICIA unrelated to the capital-based, early intervention requirements went too far in imposing costs without offsetting social benefits. In contrast, the authors and participants were divided on the wisdom of both the higher capital standards and the prompt corrective action provisions designed to enforce them. With a few exceptions, academic analysts and current and former policymakers were supportive, while consultants and bankers were critical. All agreed, however, that one year later, the banking industry was in much better financial shape than it had been when FDICIA was first enacted. Whether that trend continues depends on the steps regulators and policymakers take in the post-FDICIA environment.

Background of the Act: Intellectual and Political History

GEORGE G. KAUFMAN AND GEORGE J. BENSTON

The Intellectual History of the Federal Deposit Insurance Corporation Improvement Act of 1991

The Federal Deposit Insurance Corporation Improvement Act (FDICIA) was passed by Congress in November 1991 and signed by President Bush in December. The act promises to be the most important banking legislation since the Banking Act of 1933, yet it is also one of the most misunderstood and controversial laws enacted in recent years. As is true for much legislation, the act is long, sweeping in coverage, and complex. At first cut, it can be divided into five major parts: (1) deposit insurance reform to correct the existing perverse incentive structure, (2) recapitalization of the FDIC, (3) consumer and related regulations, (4) supervision of domestic offices of foreign banks, and (5) "bank bashing." This paper traces the intellectual history of the underpinnings of only the deposit insurance reform provisions of the act, which may be classified under the heading "structured early intervention and resolution" (SEIR). These provisions are significantly different from most deposit insurance reform proposals suggested at the time the act was being considered. Because they are not as well understood as most of the other proposals, which have been circulating longer, and will greatly affect banking for many years to come, it is useful to identify the heritage of these provisions to increase the understanding of why and how they might be expected to work.

Deposit insurance reform is achieved in the act through a combination of four provisions: (1) higher capital ratios, (2) timely, prespecified, and structured corrective actions by regulators in the affairs of financially troubled institutions, (3) prompt resolution of failing institutions before their capital becomes negative (closure rule), and (4) risk-based deposit insurance premiums. By themselves, none of these provisions are either new or likely to be effective; what is new and what makes the act different and potentially effective is the combination of all four.

WEAKNESSES IN DEPOSIT INSURANCE

Before federal deposit insurance, capital was seen as the primary protection for depositors, and banks held significantly higher capital ratios. Indeed, banks prominently displayed signs in their front windows stating "Capital and Surplus $XX Million." After enactment of insurance, this was replaced by "Member FDIC or FSLIC." Bank capital as a percent of assets declined as depositors became less concerned that it was needed to protect their funds.

Timely intervention has always been the responsibility of the supervisors or regulators. But after deposit insurance reduced the fear of runs and thereby also reduced market discipline, regulators did not pick up all the slack. Penalties were not imposed on the regulators for delayed or ineffective intervention.

Nor were there provisions for the prompt resolution of institutions that failed to respond to the intervention. Regulators had long understood that if an institution could be resolved before its economic or market value net worth became negative, no loss to depositors or the FDIC would result. But the decision to close an institution rested with the chartering agency, which did not bear the cost of the financial losses to the FDIC. Furthermore, regulators could not effectively resolve institutions until the book value of their net worth was negative. Nevertheless, until the early 1980s, at least commercial bank regulators generally resolved institutions near the time they became economically insolvent, resulting in small, if any, losses to the FDIC. This practice was abetted by two factors. First, until interest rates increased dramatically in the late 1970s, the market and book values of bank assets and liabilities did not differ greatly. Second, the small number of insolvencies in this period did not bring strong political pressure to bear on the regulators to delay resolution.

Premiums on deposit insurance were set as a fixed percent of a bank's total deposits. This did not penalize banks for risk taking to the same extent as interest rates charged by uninsured depositors. Risk-based deposit insurance premiums, similar to the premium structure of private insurance companies, had been prominently suggested at the time federal deposit insurance was first enacted in 1933, but were not adopted. In the late 1960s, Thomas Mayer and Kenneth Scott published articles in favor of such a structure. Thereafter, risk-based premiums were supported by most academics and in studies sponsored by both the FDIC and the Federal Home Loan Bank Board.

Unfortunately, neither effective timely regulatory intervention and failure resolution nor risk-adjusted insurance premiums were in place in the early 1980s. As has been well documented, the federal deposit insurance agencies had underpriced their insurance and permitted banks to operate with lower capital ratios and riskier asset and liability portfolios than they would have maintained in the absence of insurance. Consequently, banks could not absorb large adverse shocks without depleting their capital. Moreover, the sharp increase in the number of seriously troubled institutions in the mid-1980s changed the regulators' resolution practice substantially. As they became overwhelmed by the extraordinary number of troubled and failing institutions, regulators increasingly failed both to impose their discretionary sanctions either as harshly as necessary or in the time required and to enforce even the weak closure rule of zero book value capital. They frequently found it in their best interests to deny the existence of serious bank problems in the hopes that they would reverse themselves or would not worsen catastrophically until later, on someone else's watch. As a result, some economically insolvent or weak institutions were provided with both the incentive and the time to gamble for resurrection. But many of these gambles did not pay off and instead created losses for the insurer and, in the case of the thrifts, also for taxpayers.

At the same time, the regulators also came under increasing political pressure from some of their constituents, Congress, and the administration to delay closing "important" institutions on the belief that credit availability and employment in local communities would be disrupted. Indeed, some forbearance was legally mandated by the 1987 Competitive Equality Banking Act (CEBA). In an environment in which federal deposit insurance protected depositors from losses if they maintained or even increased their deposits at troubled institutions, resolution frequently occurred only after the banks' net worths were substantially negative for a considerable period of time. In sum, the institutions succumbed to problems of moral hazard and the regulators to problems of agency.

As a result of these deficiencies, when the magnitude of adverse macroeconomic shocks increased sharply in the 1980s, bank failures and losses also increased sharply. Between 1980 and 1991, some 1,400 insolvent banks and 1,100 insolvent savings and loan associations were resolved, and many more awaited resolution. Losses at resolved institutions equaled nearly 30 percent of assets, and aggregate losses to the insurance funds totaled almost $300 billion. For savings and loans, the losses at resolved institutions exceeded the resources of the Federal Savings and Loan Insurance Corporation (FSLIC) and were shifted to the taxpaying public. For commercial banks, the losses also appear to have exceeded the existing resources of the bank insurance fund (BIF) and, at minimum, will be financed by borrowing against projected future premium income.

THE SCHOLARLY ANTECEDENTS OF SEIR

The first analysis of the importance of a closure rule in minimizing FDIC losses that distinguished between bank failure per se and losses to the FDIC was published by Paul Horvitz in 1980. He argued that the appropriate role of bank examination was not to prevent failures, but to detect them early enough "so that the bank can be closed before its losses exceed the amount of its capital." This idea was expanded and developed into a closure rule by G. O. Bierwag and George Kaufman in a 1983 paper prepared for a Federal Home Loan Bank Board Task Force that, pursuant to the Garn-St Germain Depository Institutions Act of 1982, analyzed federal deposit insurance and prepared a report to Congress. Horvitz also served as a member of the task force.

Bierwag and Kaufman noted that if institutions could be resolved before their market value net worth became negative, losses to the FDIC effectively would be zero and insurance premiums could be reduced to amounts required to cover only monitoring and operations costs. Moreover, they argued that deposit insurance was not like most other types of insurance, such as life or accident insurance. Losses to the insurer were not largely "an act of God," outside its control. The deposit insurer could control its losses by controlling the timing of the resolution of insolvent institutions. Thus resolving an institution no later than when its capital declined to zero was a desirable closure rule, which was also recommended by an American Banking Association Academic Task Force in 1986.

The question was how to implement a zero net worth closure rule effectively. As noted earlier, largely because of deposit insurance, banks held extremely low levels of capital and even small adverse shocks could quickly turn a bank's capital negative before the regulators could resolve it. Moreover, deposit insurance eliminated the role of deposit withdrawals in closing insolvent or near insolvent institutions. This was the problem faced by George Benston and George Kaufman as members of an American Enterprise Institute Task Force on financial regulation reform in 1986–87. They searched for a solution that could be achieved effectively within the existing basic banking and safety net structures and was politically as well as economically feasible. Thus they rejected solutions that involved reregulation or severe structural changes, such as eliminating deposit insurance and narrow banks.

THE BENSTON-KAUFMAN PROPOSAL

Benston and Kaufman "solved" the problem by superimposing on the closure rule a structure requiring higher capital levels and early intervention by the regulators on a progressively harsher and more mandatory basis as a bank's condition deteriorates through a prescribed series of capital tranches. The system of structured early regulatory intervention was designed to change the incentives confronting both banks and regulators. In an environment of limited market discipline, capital-impaired banks would be discouraged from deteriorating further by increasing the cost to them of poor performance and, at minimum, slowing their deterioration, if not reversing it altogether.

By requiring progressively more mandatory and timely sanctions as an institution deteriorated through the capital categories, the proposal, in effect, codified actions the regulators generally undertook, although too frequently on a delayed and leisurely basis that reduced their effectiveness. The regulatory sanctions substituted for similar market sanctions that would have occurred absent deposit insurance. If, however, these sanctions failed to stem a bank's decline, the regulators would be required to resolve it at some low but positive level of capital, before its market value net worth reached zero. Federal deposit insurance coverage would remain at the existing $100,000 level, and would be enforced de facto to intensify market discipline by larger depositors. Importantly, subordinated debt would be counted fully as capital to reduce the cost of capital to institutions, to strengthen market discipline, and to provide early warnings of problems to both bankers and regulators.

The small positive capital level would provide protection to the FDIC in case of inadequate monitoring, abrupt losses, and deteriorations in a bank's capital or miscomputation of a bank's economic capital. Current shareholders would be accorded first the right to recapitalize their bank when its capital declined to the resolution trip wire. If they did not exercise this right, presumably because they believed the bank to be economically worth less than this amount, and chose to have the bank taken over by the FDIC, they would be paid the net value the FDIC received for the institution from a sale, merger, or liquidation. Thus there would be no expropriation of private capital. Moreover, to the extent the structured regulatory intervention was effective, few banks would be expected to deteriorate through all the tranches, so that there would be few new failures and FDIC takeovers.

In their proposal, Benston and Kaufman proposed four capital tranches and developed hypothetical examples of the appropriate sanctions when each tranche was breached. The lower thresholds of each tranche were tied to the current (market) value of a bank's capital at 10, 6, and 3 percent of total assets. Resolution would be required at 3 percent. The sanctions included restrictions on growth, interaffiliate transactions, dividend payments, interest payments to subordinated debtholders, and product powers, and would be harsher in the lower capital tranches. The sanctions would be mostly discretionary with the regulators in the higher capital tranches and become progressively less discretionary as a bank's capital fell into the lower tranches.

SEIR was designed to introduce a carrot as well as a stick approach to bank behavior, providing not only penalties for poor performance, but rewards for good performance. Banks maintaining sufficiently high capital levels would be rewarded with broader product powers, less intense supervision, and greater managerial freedom. Thus institutions would be encouraged to achieve and maintain the top capital tranche. As summarized by Benston and Kaufman, the advantages of SEIR included

—improved bank performance and a much smaller number of bank failures;

—lower losses to the FDIC from failures;

—lower insurance premiums to pay for FDIC losses;

—equal treatment of depositors at failed banks of all sizes and importance and the termination of "too big to fail";

—reduced need for prudential regulations in the long run;

—reduced need for restrictions on bank activities that could be adequately monitored by the insurer; and

—exertion of market force discipline through uninsured depositors, subordinated debtholders, and shareholders.

Indeed, because banks would be resolved with no or only small negative net worth, losses to uninsured depositors would be zero or small and deposit insurance effectively would be redundant. This is why SEIR is considered deposit insurance reform.

INITIAL RESPONSE TO THE PROPOSAL

Although Benston and Kaufman were the primary authors of the proposal, it benefited substantially from the input and comments of the other members of the American Enterprise Institute Task Force and also of the members of the associated Advisory Committee, in particular Thomas Huertas of Citicorp. The proposal was first presented publicly at an AEI conference in November 1987 in Washington, D.C., at which the task force reported their conclusions and recommendations. In early 1988, it was published in draft form in the Staff Memoranda Series of the Federal Reserve Bank of Chicago. The final form was published in the Monograph Series in Finance and Economics by the Salomon Brothers Center for the Study of Financial Institutions at New York University and, in a shorter version, as a chapter in the official report of the project published by AEI. In December 1988, Kaufman presented the proposal at the annual conference on savings and loan issues sponsored by the Federal Home Loan Bank of San Francisco.

First reactions were mixed. At the American Enterprise Institute conference, the proposal was supported by both Paul Horvitz, who was a discussant of the proposal, and Allan Meltzer, who commented on the overall task force report. However, the proposal was mildly criticized by Stanley Silverberg and severely criticized by John Kareken, the other discussants. Meltzer concluded, "I believe the AEI recommendations would be improved if the explicit recommendations of the Benston and Kaufman study were incorporated, with some amendments and extensions." Horvitz noted that "there is agreement that optimal closure policy is a crucial element in the supervisory system. This rather obvious point does not appear in the older deposit insurance literature." Silverberg agreed with the general thrust of the proposal and policy recommendations, but stated that "in the real world, some of what Benston and Kaufman advocate would be more difficult to implement than they suggest, and the cost and failure reductions would be less dramatic."

On the other hand, Kareken concluded that "Benston and Kaufman rely on a proposition that in general has been shown to be false: that the probability that a depository institution will fail decreases as equity capital increases." Moreover, "timely reorganization, arguably a confiscation of private property, could . . . be illegal." As a result, "the policy advocated by Benston and Kaufman is not nearly as practical or workable as they make out."

At the Federal Home Loan Bank of San Francisco conference, the three discussants were also skeptical. William Isaac, former chairman of the FDIC, argued that there was nothing new in the proposal: this was the way the FDIC has always operated. Richard Syron, then president of the Federal Home Loan Bank of Boston and currently president of the Federal Reserve Bank of Boston, was unhappy with the provision that institutions with the highest capital would be subject to only "minimum supervision." Lastly, Larry White, a member of the Federal Home Loan Bank Board at the time, argued that the proposal should focus on risk-based capital, not on total capital: "The regulators should address risk directly rather than trying to build excessively high capital walls around it."

In December 1988, the SEIR proposal was refined and endorsed by the Shadow Financial Regulatory Committee, and, in early 1989, by a Task Force on Depository Institutions Reform of the Brookings Institution, both of which included Benston and Kaufman as members. Members of both groups discussed SEIR at banking and academic meetings, with Congress through testimony at hearings and personal contact with congressmen and their staffs, and with bank regulators and the Treasury Department through personal contacts. The prompt closing of troubled institutions as soon as their own capital funds were depleted greatly appealed to a Congress under strong political pressure from the public for the extraordinarily large losses in the S&L industry that were perceived to be caused by regulatory inaction and political favoritism.

The influential General Accounting Office and Congressional Budget Office both supported the underlying thrust of SEIR. On the other hand, the mandatory and automatic features of the SEIR proposal as well as the emphasis on market values were strongly opposed by both the regulators and the administration, who had confidence in their ability to choose between troubled institutions that might succeed or fail. In addition, they feared that the reduction in their discretion and flexibility would reduce their own power, influence, and visibility.

Nor was there much support from the majority of the academic community. Their attention was focused primarily on eliminating government deposit insurance altogether or, at minimum, rolling back account coverage to well below $100,000; on introducing risk-based insurance premiums, priced generally on the basis of the output of option-pricing models; and on establishing more restrictive and fail-safe narrow banks. Indeed, not a single research article on SEIR appeared in a major academic finance or economic journal by authors not associated with the Shadow or other groups that had endorsed the proposal through 1991, nor did such authors present papers on this proposal at academic conferences. In part, this may have reflected the fact that elegant proofs, which might justify publication in prestigious academic journals, were not required to demonstrate that resolution of institutions before the market value of net worth turned negative would accrue losses only to shareholders and not to depositors or the FDIC. Others questioned why regulators or Congress would obey the constraints on their behavior when both had violated the spirit of the existing regulations so frequently and enthusiastically.

LEGISLATIVE ADOPTION

Nevertheless, in the fall of 1990 much of the SEIR proposal was incorporated in a bill introduced by Donald Riegle, chairman of the Senate Banking Committee (S. 3103 and S. 543). In January 1991, similar provisions were introduced in a bill by Henry Gonzalez, chairman of the House Banking Committee (H.R. 6). In February 1991, the general thrust of the proposal was included among the recommendations in the major study *Modernizing the Financial System*, published by the U.S. Treasury Department, and in the legislation that it recommended to Congress the next month (H.R. 1505 and S. 713).

The SEIR proposal of Benston-Kaufman, the Shadow Financial Regulatory Committee, and the Brookings Task Force was modified somewhat in these bills. The number of tranches or categories was increased from four to five and the mandatory nature of the sanctions in the lower tranches, the emphasis on market values, and the universality

TABLE 1. *Calculating Hypothetical Bank Insurance Fund (BIF) Loss Exposure from Asset Breakdown Given by Veribanc's Partition of FDIC-Insured Commercial and Savings Banks, as of June 30, 1992*[a]

Veribanc category	Number of banks	Assets (billions of dollars)	Hypothetical rate of case resolution	Hypothetical assets to be resolved (billions of dollars)	Hypothetical rate of BIF loss	Hypothetical BIF loss exposure (billions of dollars)
Red: no stars	143	34.4	0.9	31.0	0.3	9.3
Yellow: no stars	99	28.8	0.9	26.0	0.3	7.8
Yellow: one star	155	225.0	0.6	135.0	0.2	27.0
Yellow: two stars	639	166.8	0.6	100.0	0.2	20.0
Green: no stars	28	8.1	0.4	3.2	0.2	0.6
Green: one star	3	54.4	0.4	21.8	0.2	4.4
Total "doubtful" banks	1,067	517.5	...	317.0	...	69.1
Green: two stars	1,277	54.4	0.005	0.3	0.2	0.1
Green: three stars	9,801	2,650.7	0.001	2.7	0.2	0.5
Total banks	12,145	3,222.6	...	320.0	...	69.7
Less BIF's reserve for its estimated liability for unresolved cases						15.2
BIF's unbooked loss exposure						54.5

a. The hypothetical rates of needed case resolution and of BIF loss are offered as indicative guesses. Detailed analysis of past transitions across partitions of bank assets would be needed to establish econometric estimates of these variables.

of the prompt resolution to all banks regardless of size or importance were weakened, particularly in the Treasury's bill. In addition, one or more of the congressional bills included provisions for risk-based insurance premiums, expanding risk-based capital to account for interest rate and credit concentration risk, and restrictions on Federal Reserve discount window lending to troubled institutions. The bills also included features not directly related to deposit insurance reform, such as permitting banks additional product and geographic powers, provisions intended to increase consumer protection, and recapitalization of the FDIC.

The final FDIC Improvement Act was crafted by a Senate-House Conference Committee in November 1991, as Congress was adjourning for the session, just four years after SEIR's initial unveiling (see appendix to this chapter). The act maintained the thrust of the original Benston-Kaufman proposal, but weakened it sufficiently so that deposit insurance is unlikely to be viewed as redundant. Moreover, by not expanding bank powers, the act weakened the potential carrots available to highly capitalized banks and weakened bank profitability in general. Nevertheless, the primary thrust of the act was to reduce the costs of bank insolvencies to near zero (see table 1). The act delegates to the bank regulators the responsibility both for interpreting many of the provisions and for designing and implementing the rules and regulations. Thus the regulators have the opportunity to weaken, distort, and even sabotage the intent of the legislation.

Indeed, many of the regulations proposed or adopted to date by the bank and thrift regulatory agencies appear to weaken the effectiveness of the act.

—The highest of the five prompt corrective action tranches or categories, termed "well capitalized," has been defined to include more than 90 percent of all banks holding nearly two-thirds of all bank assets in June 1992, and 98 percent of all banks holding 97 percent of all bank assets were classified as "adequately capitalized," even though 8 percent of all banks holding 14 percent of total assets were on the FDIC's problem bank list at that time.

—The spread between insurance premiums on the best and worst banks has been set at only eight basis points, a much smaller difference than that set by the market on CD rates of banks of differing credit quality.

—Only some 20 percent of all institutions will be required to hold additional capital against their interest rate risk exposure in amounts that are both substantially inadequate and not sensitive to future un-recognized market value losses from adverse rate changes.

On the other hand, at least four adopted or proposed regulations strengthen the carrot-stick strategy of the act. Insurance premiums and restrictions on the ability of banks to attract brokered deposit, to attract interbank and correspondent funds and thereby incur credit exposure to other banks, and to offer pass-through insurance coverage on em-ployee benefit plans are tied to a bank's capital position. The higher is a bank's capital, the lower are its insurance premiums and the fewer and milder are the restrictions on its activities. These regulations should and already are encouraging banks to increase their capital po-sitions to qualify for the highest capital tranche. Banks are raising ex-ternal capital at a record pace and the ratio of book value equity to assets in June 1992 was the highest since the mid-1960s. It should be noted, however, that while the risk-based insurance premiums rein-force SEIR, they would be far less effective without an effective clo-sure rule.

As noted earlier, FDICIA also contains a number of provisions other than deposit insurance reform that, for good or bad, impose numerous additional restrictions and reporting burdens on banks. Unfortunately the response to these provisions by banks, regulators, and the adminis-tration has been sufficiently negative to have distracted attention away from the more positive and important deposit insurance reform provis-ions. This reaction has helped cause both a misunderstanding of the primary purpose of the act and a downgrading of its perceived impor-tance, although it promises to shape significantly the efficiency, profit-ability, and safety of banking for many years to come. Indeed, FDICIA promises to permit bankers to reclaim their institutions from excessive government intervention and micromanagement by increasing their capital to levels more consistent with those of their noninsured com-petitors. If successful, banking may be able to halt its slide toward becoming a public utility. If unsuccessful, and banks again encounter solvency problems that threaten taxpayer involvement, more radical congressional surgery that would be far less favorable to banks, such as narrow banking and more government micromanagement, is likely.

Federal Deposit Insurance Corporation Improvement Act of 1991: Implementation Timetable for Deposit Insurance Reform Providers, with Latest Permissible Date

December 19, 1992 (immediately)

Least cost resolution (141)—resolution at last present value cost to FDIC.

Early resolution (143)—encourages early resolution of troubled institutions at least long-term cost to FDIC.

Foreign deposits (312)—prohibits protection with exceptions.

June 19, 1992

Brokered deposits (301)—restricts and prohibits use by non-well-capitalized institutions. Imposed June 16, 1992.

December 19, 1992

Accounting objectives, standards, and requirements (121)—requires accurate reports, including market values to extent feasible.

Prompt corrective action (131)—establishes five capital categories for regulatory action, including resolution at 2 percent tangible equity capital, and requires report on "material" losses to FDIC.

Conservatorship and receivership to facilitate prompt regulatory action (133)—expands grounds for regulatory resolution.

Interbank liabilities (308)—limits interbank risk exposure to reduce systemic risk potential.

June 19, 1993

Improving capital standards (305)—regulators to require sufficient capital to prevent loss to FDIC and to facilitate prompt corrective action, including accounting for interest rate risk and concentration of credit risk.

December 1, 1993

Standards for safety and soundness (132)—requires regulatory standards regarding (1) operations and management; (2) asset quality, earnings, and stock valuation; and (3) compensation.

December 19, 1993

Federal Reserve discount window advances (142)—restricts loans to undercapitalized and critically undercapitalized institutions.

January 1, 1994

Risk-based assessments (302)—FDIC establishes risk-scaled premiums. Imposed January 1, 1993.

January 1, 1995

Least cost resolution (141)—prohibits protecting uninsured depositors with exception for declaration of systemic risk by FDIC with approval of Federal Reserve and Treasury (president). Costs of application of exception paid by special levy on bank assets.

ROBERT R. GLAUBER

FDICIA: The Wheels Came Off on the Road through Congress

I have the—not entirely pleasant—task of discussing the legislative history of FDICIA, which bears at least some resemblance to the Treasury proposal outlined in the February 1991 report, *Modernizing the Financial System*.[1] The seed of the Treasury proposal was planted in the fall of 1990, when the domestic policy staff embarked upon a protracted series of seminars on banking within Treasury. Unfortunately, the final fruit of this seed can best be characterized as a relative of Rosemary's baby—missing some important limbs and having others with strange deformities. But perhaps that is too negative. There is, in fact, much in FDICIA that is good policy, most importantly the recognition that capital forms the basis for a strong and healthy banking system. And the attempt to broaden what banks can do and where they can do it has elevated these issues to a national debate, laying the groundwork for changes that will make U.S. banks more competitive.

Today the banking industry is far healthier than it was in late 1990, when many important banks were close to the edge and senior regulators were seriously worried. Responding to the FDICIA's requirements and incentives to add capital, the industry has recapitalized, preparing itself to finance the next expansion and to take advantage of the broader products and activities that many believe are bound to come. Thus far in 1992 banks have raised $39 billion in debt and equity capital.[2] As a result, the industry has more equity capital today than at any time since 1966 and 93 percent of banks meet the new "well capitalized" standard.[3]

DEPOSIT INSURANCE REFORM IS NOT ENOUGH

The Treasury report and its companion legislation are the product of the 1989 S&L legislation (FIRREA), which mandated that Treasury and

33

the banking agencies complete a deposit insurance study by February 1991. Treasury concluded that deposit insurance reform, while vital, is not enough. Banks, protected by deposit insurance from the discipline of the marketplace, were making riskier loans—classic moral hazard behavior. But the incentive to take risks comes from a secular decline in bank profitability and a loss of market position in the financial services industry. Bank return on equity has fallen from 12.2 percent in the last half of the 1970s to 8.6 percent in the 1985–91 period; depository institutions share of the financial asset market has fallen from 55 percent to 36 percent in the same period.[4]

Changes in the competitive structure of the financial services industry—new technology and increased sophistication of the capital markets—have cost banks profitability and competitive position. Twenty-five years ago banks had the financial services playing field pretty much to themselves. Today it is very crowded. Automobile companies through finance subsidiaries (for example, GMAC, Ford Credit) offer auto loans to consumers nationwide. Fidelity and other mutual fund groups offer nationwide deposit and checking accounts through money market mutual funds. Merrill Lynch offers mortgages nationwide, while General Electric, through General Electric Credit Corporation, makes small business loans nationwide. And Goldman, Sachs offers commercial paper—the equivalent of bank loans for large, high quality corporations—nationwide. Confronting this competition, banks are prohibited from operating branches across state lines and generally from dealing in securities.

Structural changes such as these require structural reform. Deposit insurance reform alone will not do the job. Changes in the laws regulating what banks can do are needed to make banks healthy and competitively viable.

Reform of deposit insurance must proceed on many fronts, including measures to enhance shareholder discipline (for example, risk-based insurance premiums), depositor discipline (for example, limits on the size and types of accounts insured), restrictions on the assets that can be funded by insured deposits, and private deposit insurance. Treasury concluded that no single measure would be sufficient. None are new, all having been thoroughly discussed.[5]

At the heart of virtually all the deposit insurance reforms is required capital, the foundation of the proposal. As the Treasury report stated, "The single most powerful tool to make banks safer is capital. It is an "up-front" cushion to absorb losses ahead of the taxpayer, and banks are less likely to take excessive risk when they have substantial amounts of their own money at risk."[6] Private markets rely primarily on capital to control default risk; deposit insurance reform should as well. To avoid setting stifling levels of required capital, the proposal in places offered an incentive (carrot) to hold more capital in exchange for enhanced activities, lower deposit insurance costs, and reduced regulatory burden. Linked to capital was the prompt corrective action mechanisms discussed in detail in the Benston and Kaufman paper in this volume.[7]

THREE FUNDAMENTAL STRUCTURAL CHANGES

Treasury proposed three fundamental structural changes. The first was repeal of the McFadden Act to permit nationwide branching for national banks, subject to state control of intrastate activities. With forty-nine states now permitting interstate *banking* through holding company affiliates, it is time to reap the efficiency benefits of interstate *branching*. Economists may dispute the cost savings available from consolidation, but nearly $3 billion a year has already been saved from mergers such as Chemical–Manufacturers Hanover, NCNB–Citizei s & Southern, and Bank of America–Security Pacific.[8] And consul' ants (perhaps a biased source) estimate the savings could run as high as $15 billion a year.[9] Whatever the cost savings, nationwide banking will reduce risk by encouraging more geographically diversified loan portfolios. It will be unlikely that the Texas banking experience, where nine of the ten largest banks failed in the energy bust of the early 1980s, will be repeated.

The second structural change was repeal of the Glass-Steagall Act and modification of the Bank Holding Company Act of 1956 to permit a bank to affiliate through a holding company with firms engaged in a broad range of financial services, including securities underwriting, mutual fund management, and insurance underwriting. Securities underwriting simply allows banks to continue to serve their large corporate customers as securitization encourages them to migrate from bank loans to debt securities. Securities underwriting should be a profitable business for some banks; investment banking is one of the most concentrated and profitable businesses, earning more than 20 percent return on equity, which has amounted to some $6 billion before taxes in each of the last two years.[10] Expanded mutual fund and insurance activities would allow banks to sell more products through their fixed-cost distribution systems. Can bank safety and competitive fairness be maintained when bank activities are expanded? The answer is yes. Firewalls would limit loans from banks to affiliates and customers, but the strongest firewall would be capital: only highly capitalized banks would be permitted to enjoy broader activities.

Finally, commercial ownership of banks, through modification of the Bank Holding Company Act, would provide capital, management talent, and discipline. Perhaps of more importance, it would provide a pathway for resources to exit an industry plagued by chronic excess capacity. If returns are unsatisfactory, a diversified company is more likely to close down its bank subsidiary than a stand-alone bank is to voluntarily close itself down.

The combination of reforms were intended to have two broad effects. First, they would resize and reshape an industry that is strikingly and dysfunctionally fragmented. The 11,500 banks in the United States, compared with 200–300 in Britain and Germany, amount to fifty banks per million people versus six banks per million people in the other two countries.[11] For the United States this has meant recurrent excess capacity and operating inefficiencies leading to destructive competition in lending to ever less credit-worthy customers. Second, the reforms would allow banks to compete with other financial services companies for the profitable business they have lost, including securities underwriting, mutual fund management, and insurance product sales.

THE POLITICAL REALITIES OF REFORM LEGISLATION

So much for the intellectual niceties, what about the politics of the Treasury proposal? The proposed legislation had to pass review by eight congressional committees, where it ultimately faced more than one thousand amendments. Powerful forces were arrayed against the administration. First and foremost, the structural changes were viewed as deregulation, which many saw as having caused the S&L debacle. Congress was embarrassed by the S&L experience and ready to pile restrictive regulations on the banks. Second, the chairmen of both Senate and House banking committees wanted a "narrow" bill, including deposit insurance but no structural reforms. Both had introduced narrow bills before Treasury put forward its legislation.[12] And Chairman John Dingell of the House Energy and Commerce Committee had consistently blocked Glass-Steagall repeal, most recently in the fall of 1988. And finally there were the industry lobbies: the powerful securities and insurance lobbies opposed to reform and the banking lobby unable to coalesce in support of a broad, coherent reform package.

On the other hand, the administration did have a few forces on its side. The banking industry was in crisis and the bank insurance fund had to be recapitalized by the end of 1991. The usual argument, "If it ain't broke, don't fix it," clearly did not apply. A banking bill, to replenish the insurance fund at the minimum was necessary, and the need for structural reform was hard for many to deny. Also, Treasury had succeeded in getting the support of all the banking regulatory agencies to a degree unprecedented in recent history.[13]

The Treasury report and draft legislation were greeted with skepticism in the press and on Capitol Hill. The legislation was pronounced "dead on arrival." Even those who intellectually supported the package said it was too large and too broad to succeed politically. Treasury was criticized for making all three structural reforms—interstate branching, Glass-Steagall repeal, and commercial ownership—part of the package.

In fact, it would have been impossible politically to get a narrower package of reforms—say, interstate branching alone—out of the starting gate because of an earlier bit of history. The Senate would not act on banking legislation before the House did. The Senate had passed the Proxmire Financial Modernization Act of 1988 repealing Glass-Steagall by 94–2 only to watch it die when Chairman Dingell refused to take it up in the House. So the House Banking Committee would have to act first this time.

In the House committee the dominant support for the administration's bill came from the bipartisan Bank Study Group, led by Congressman Doug Bernard. The foundation of this group's policy position was commercial ownership. (In fact, late in the process Bernard opposed a House bill containing interstate branching but not commercial ownership.) At the same time the strongest industry group supporting the administration legislation was the Financial Services Council, whose members (Ford, Citicorp, American Express, Sears, Bankers Trust, John Hancock, among others) have as their first priorities Glass-Steagall repeal and commercial ownership. Interstate branching alone would get nowhere in the House Banking Committee. Moreover, to allow banks into financial services but not to allow diversified financial services companies (many of which are legally "commercial firms") would be both unfair and politically unbalanced. Glass-Steagall repeal had to be linked to commercial ownership.

THE LEGISLATIVE JOURNEY

During May and June the House Banking Committee considered the administration's legislation. To the surprise of many, first the Financial Institutions Subcommittee and then the full committee voted out bills that contained all the essential deposit insurance and structural reform components of the Treasury bill—interstate branching, Glass-Steagall repeal, and commercial ownership. The votes were 36–0 in the subcommittee and a bipartisan 31–20 majority in the full committee.

Reacting to these votes, the press swung all the way from "dead on arrival" to "now impossible to lose." Nothing could have been further from the truth. The voices of the Energy and Commerce Committee and Chairman Dingell had yet to be heard. And now all the lobbies opposed to the bill—securities industry, insurance industry, and small, country banks—were geared up for a serious fight.

On the Senate side the Banking Committee voted out a bill in early August containing interstate branching and Glass-Steagall repeal but not commercial ownership. The 12–9 vote was bipartisan but very much divided, foreshadowing a long delay in getting to the Senate floor.

Back in the House, Speaker Thomas Foley had directed the Energy and Commerce Committee to report out a bill by the end of September, refusing to accede to Chairman Dingell's request for a delay until February. Under pressure from all sides, Energy and Commerce produced landmark legislation: a bill repealing Glass-Steagall. But the terms of the bill were a step backward in many directions: excessively restrictive firewalls controlling securities activities, unreasonable restraints on bank insurance sales, and the threat of regulatory gridlock from re-carving regulatory turf in favor of the SEC (and the Energy and Commerce Committee). Henry Gonzalez, Chairman of the House Banking Committee, and Chairman Dingell then agreed to bring to the floor a bill containing deposit insurance reform, interstate branching, and Glass-Steagall repeal based on the Energy and Commerce bill, but omitting commercial ownership. The administration announced it would seek to strip out the Glass-Steagall provisions on the floor, leaving interstate branching as the sole structural reform. If it failed, the administration would oppose the entire bill.

The bill made it to the House floor on October 31, with the full support of Chairman Dingell. While the administration narrowly failed to strip out the Glass-Steagall provisions, interstate branching was affirmed overwhelmingly, 366–4. But on final passage, with the administration opposed and the banking industry split, the House defeated the bill. A week later the House passed a narrow bill containing only deposit insurance reform and a recapitalization of the insurance fund.

Confronted with the House's refusal to pass structural reform, the Senate several days later nevertheless debated, and ultimately passed by voice vote, a bill containing interstate branching, as well as provisions similar to the House bill, despite the less than enthusiastic support of the banking industry. With only days remaining before adjournment, the leadership of the House and Senate met in the Speaker's office to determine whether the House conferees would be given instructions to agree with the Senate to adopt interstate branching. The House had already overwhelmingly passed the interstate branching provisions on the way to rejecting the broad bill. But despite the fact that bank branching falls beyond the jurisdiction of the Energy and Commerce Committee, Chairman Dingell objected to the adoption of branching provisions unless either his restrictive Glass-Steagall amendments were also included or there was a moratorium on further bank securities activities under current law. His objection doomed the chance to include interstate branching in the final legislation, which was written several days later in conference.

THE FINAL FDICIA: TOO MUCH AND TOO LITTLE

As finally passed, FDICIA breaks new ground in according capital the same central role in a regulated industry that it plays in a market economy. Capital sets the standard for early regulatory intervention and resolution. And it provides an incentive for lower deposit insurance costs and broader permitted activities.

However, in its interventionist zeal Congress added greatly to the burden of excessive regulatory micromanagement and paperwork reporting. The early intervention trip wires now include standards for back-office operations and minimum market-to-book-value ratios, as well as the capital standards proposed by Treasury. Auditors are now directed to be the policemen of safety and soundness laws. And a bank must give ninety-days' notice before it can close an automatic teller machine.

But the greatest defect of FDICIA is the omission of the structural reforms—interstate branching, broader permitted activities, and commercial ownership—that are essential if banks are to be competitive in modern financial markets. There are many reasons for this failure, but ranking high is the inability of the banking industry to coalesce around a position in support of these changes, while the industry's competitors are effectively united in opposition.

The original Treasury proposal traveled much further than most observers believed possible. A bill to make banks more competitive by broadening permitted activities and enabling interstate branching came very close to passage; indeed, interstate branching passed the Senate. The groundwork has been laid. But if the banking industry is to achieve long-run competitive viability, it will have to play a more effective role in support of its own interests.

NOTES

1. U.S. Department of the Treasury, *Modernizing the Financial System: Recommendations for Safer, More Competitive Banks* (1991).

2. "Strong Profits Take the Sting Out of Newest Capital Rules," *American Banker*, December 1, 1992, p. 1.

3. Ibid.

4. Return on equity figures are from U.S. Bureau of the Census, *Statistical Abstract of the United States*, various editions; market share figures are from Salomon Brothers, *Comments on Credit*, October 16, 1992, p. 2.

5. A good discussion of deposit insurance reform proposals is contained in William S. Haraf and Rose Marie Kushmeider, eds., *Restructuring Banking and Financial Services in America* (Washington: American Enterprise Institute, 1988).

6. U.S. Department of the Treasury, *Modernizing the Financial System*, p. 12.

7. Benston and Kaufman use the phrase "structured early intervention and resolution."

8. Jeffrey A. Clark, "Economies of Scale and Scope at Depository Financial Institutions: A Review of the Literature," *Federal Reserve Bank of Kansas City Economic Review,* September–October, 1988, pp. 16–33, contains an excellent summary of the literature.

9. See, for example, Larry Mendonca, "Done Right, Bank Mergers Can Save Money," *Wall Street Journal,* May 13, 1992, p. A14.

10. "Brokerage Firms' Outlook Is Cloudy," *New York Times,* January 4, 1993, p. D4.

11. Mendonca, "Done Right, Bank Mergers Can Save Money."

12. S. 3103 and S. 543 were introduced by Chairman Donald Riegle of the Senate Banking Committee in the fall of 1990. The original version of H.R. 6 containing only deposit insurance reform was introduced by Chairman Henry Gonzalez of the House Banking Committee in January 1991.

13. All the regulatory agencies testified in support of all major structural reforms, including Glass-Steagall repeal and commercial ownership of banks.

WILLIAM S. HARAF

Comments

It is a pleasure to participate in this volume commemorating the first anniversary of FDICIA, one of the most important and, I might add, disappointing pieces of banking legislation of the past sixty years.

Before FDICIA, the deposit insurance system was badly in need of reform, as George G. Kaufman and George J. Benston document in their paper in this volume. But the U.S. economy was also laboring along with a financial structure that was hopelessly outmoded and inefficient, a subject that the authors do not discuss. Bank charters were narrowly defined, so banks were hampered in their ability to offer the types of new products and services their customers were demanding. Interstate activities were sharply constrained. Restrictions on affiliations between banks and other financial and nonfinancial business prevented the kind of financial convergence and efficient use of capital seen in Europe and other parts of the world. And while securitization was becoming increasingly an important phenomenon, the United States had a highly concentrated, virtually oligopolistic, securities industry in which the top eight firms earned more than 80 percent of the underwriting revenues.

It was a ridiculously antiquated and inefficient financial system. The Treasury proposal was intended to bring it into the twenty-first century. The proposal struck a careful balance between shoring up the safety and soundness of the banking system and needed financial modernization. Benston and Kaufman provide an exhaustive discussion of the intellectual origins of the safety and soundness components, particularly the prompt corrective action provisions.[1] They justifiably claim substantial credit for these provisions, and in my opinion they are likely to be an important reform. But the intellectual origins of the financial modernization component were also well established through a number of important books, papers, and conferences going back a decade or more, which analyzed the efficiency gains as well as the potential risks.

Despite these solid origins, the Treasury plan was considered to be a politically bold proposal from the beginning. To the surprise of many observers, it passed a crucial test in the House Banking Committee more or less intact. Then it ran into a brick wall in the form of a coalition composed of the securities industry, the insurance industry, and independent bankers, who collectively managed to bottle up and ultimately defeat the financial modernization component of the Treasury plan.

The existing structure survived not because it made economic sense, but because its beneficiaries were politically well-organized and powerful. Many securities firms, which were enjoying huge profits from their protected position in the marketplace, fiercely defended Glass-Steagall barriers to competition from commercial banks. Independent banks and a few regional banks used their grassroots networks to hold up interstate branching.[2] And the insurance industry, which was fearful of a new delivery channel for insurance products that was potentially more efficient than their existing system, pulled out all the stops to prevent banking and insurance linkages. Of course, the public debate was always couched in public policy terms—these groups expressed concerns about cross-subsidies, market power, lending to communities, and the like. Although most of their arguments could not withstand close scrutiny, they were politically effective.

At the same time, fears about another taxpayer bailout—this time of the BIF—led to a spate of additional safety and soundness rules. Deposit insurance reform was desperately needed, and there were legitimate and fundamental differences of opinion as to how to proceed. But the outcome, I believe, was a disaster for banks and for the economy. In the grand tradition of Edward Kane, let me offer an analogy to illustrate why. An elderly gentleman with a number of vague, but modestly debilitating symptoms arranges appointments to see his internist, a chiropractor, a surgeon, a dentist, a proctologist, and even a faith healer to seek advice about his health. They all recommend programs of treatment based on their training and experience. The proctologist, I might add, proposed a particularly ambitious treatment plan. Confused about the conflicting advice, he undertakes them all. Three months later, after being drugged, reamed, racked, bled, root canaled, purged, blessed, and otherwise tortured, the poor old gentleman died.

Similarly, the architects of FDICIA made sure that virtually every idea to enhance the safety and soundness of depository institutions found its way into the law—risk-based premiums, early intervention, market discipline from large depositors, Reg Q-type deposit ceilings, brokered deposit and pass-through restrictions, tougher accounting and audit standards, discount window reforms, mandatory operational and managerial standards, closer supervision, higher effective capital standards, enhanced risk-based capital standards, limits on activities of state chartered banks, and more. In addition, burdensome new consumer provisions, such as the misnamed Truth in Saving Act, were also added.[3] Many of the new regulations that found their way into FDICIA were based on sound and useful ideas. In combination, however, they could not be remotely justified by any sensible cost-benefit calculation. Judging from the experience of the elderly gentleman, the prognosis for banking is not good.

In the end, FDICIA preserved all the inefficiencies and pockets of market power associated with our highly fragmented and compartmentalized financial system, and it added to the problem by crippling the financial intermediation function in the United States. Prior to FDICIA, the deposit insurance system was genuinely overextended and in need of reform. But FDICIA was a thoughtless overreaction. It was safety and soundness overkill. Unless something is done legislatively, I believe that the cumulative effect of the vast range of new rules, each perhaps modestly burdensome but survivable on its own, will have a debilitating effect over time. Some of the costs will fall on bank shareholders, but the general public will bear most of the burden—either directly through higher prices and reduced availability for banking services, or indirectly by forcing them to use intrinsically less efficient financial services.

Even before FDICIA, depository institutions were contracting relative to the economy. For most of the 1980s, finance companies, foreign banks operating in the United States, and the securities markets grew faster than banks. In fact, it is hard to square this observation with the notion that commercial banks enjoy large subsidies from their access to the safety net. Since 1988, however, the relative shrinkage of depository credit has been much more pronounced, and for the first time it has been accompanied by a slowdown in growth of M2. A recent Federal Reserve staff study found that the rising cost of financial intermediation, including tougher capital standards and higher deposit insurance premiums, has contributed to recent unusually slow growth of M2 (or alternatively, to unusual strength in M2 velocity).[4] Rather than compete with higher-yielding nonbank investments, banks are simply allowing certain types of deposits to run off. The regulatory burdens imposed by FDICIA will raise the cost of depository intermediation further and lead to more retrenchment and more monetary and credit availability effects.

CAPITAL STANDARDS AND CREDIT AVAILABILITY

Let me focus special attention on capital-based regulation and supervision, since it is the centerpiece of FDICIA. The Treasury plan devised the concept of the well-capitalized depository institution as a carrot—such institutions were to be free of all affiliation restrictions, and their holding companies were to be free from consolidated capital requirements. Although the carrots were deleted during the legislative process, the well-capitalized concept survived. Regulatory sanctions, audit requirements, and a raft of new restrictions on interbank liabilities, deposit interest rates, brokered deposits and pass-throughs, activities of state-chartered banks, and discount window access are all keyed to an institution's capital category. FDICIA also gave regulators authority to downgrade an institution to a lower capital category based on a supervisory examination. Prudent bank management will generally want to have a capital structure that will protect them from the adverse consequences of such a downgrade. The result of this intense focus on capital-based supervision is that the 10 percent tier 1 plus tier 2, 6 percent tier 1, and 5 percent leverage thresholds for a well-capitalized bank will become the de facto minimum standards in the United States. Indeed, most banks will want to maintain a cushion above that threshold.

In a recent Federal Reserve Bank of Chicago study, Herb Baer and John McElravey found that banks were behaving as if the level of capital at which capital requirements become binding were 2 to 3 percentage points above regulatory minimums.[5] Banks with capital ratios below those levels were shrinking on average or, at a minimum, growing very slowly. They offer two possible explanations. One is that banking organizations wanted to have an extra cushion of capital to avoid the regulatory costs associated with falling below the threshold. Another is that regulators began exerting pressure on banks well before their capital ratios fell to the published regulatory minimums. The study was done using pre-FDICIA data, when the penalties for falling below required minimums were discretionary and less severe than they are now. In the post-FDICIA environment, the incentives to keep a cushion above the well-capitalized threshold are stronger—the 10 percent, 6 percent, 5 percent test as a practical matter becomes a 12 percent, 8 percent, 7 percent de facto industry standard.

Many of the distinguished banking economists represented in this volume belong to the "more is better" school of thought on capital, and I am sure they will applaud this result. There is no doubt that bank capital ratios had gotten too low by the mid-1980s, and there has been a quite impressive effort to rebuild capital ratios since then. But ever higher capital thresholds are not an unambiguous benefit. Particularly in combination with new regulatory burdens, they will force banks to further curtail credit availability and to allocate credit differently than an unregulated lender, such as a finance company, would.

The methodology for pricing loans has now become fairly standardized across both banks and nonbanks. It involves (1) rating the borrower to estimate probability of default and loss in event of default; (2) determining an equity allocation for the loan sufficient to cover possible losses on the loan at, say, a two standard deviation confidence level; and (3) pricing the loan based on the equity allocation, a return on equity target, and the marginal cost of borrowed money for the remainder.

For top-quality investment grade borrowers, the two standard deviation equity allocation is small, literally a few basis points. If the bank is required to allocate 6 percent or more equity against the loan, it will require a rate on the loan far higher than that charged by nonbank lenders and/or the securities markets. Banks simply cannot make money lending to low-risk companies with access to other sources of funds. The regulatory capital requirement for many potential loans is greater than that merited by the inherent risk of the claims. An unavoidable consequence is that the loans that remain on bank balance sheets are likely to be those for which the market's assessment of the appropriate capital allocation is greater than or equal to the regulatory assessment. Hence the higher is the capital requirement, the more banks are pushed into serving a borrowing clientele for which a relatively high equity allocation is rational. At the same time, however,

banks face a catch-22 in that there are significant supervisory constraints on their ability to serve such a borrowing clientele. So FDICIA
will accelerate the disintermediation process, and some classes of borrowers will simply not get served.

While it is fair to say that banks previously enjoyed a leverage advantage associated with the safety net, that advantage is now gone. In
the post-FDICIA environment, bank capital ratios will look like those
of most large finance companies. Banks will not have a leverage advantage and they will be subject to costly burdens their nonbank competitors do not face.

A recent Federal Bank of New York study points out that finance
companies did not suffer a big leverage disadvantage relative to banks
even during the pre-FDICIA period of the late 1980s when bank capital
ratios were lower than they are today.[6] The ratio of equity plus subordinated debt to assets for GE Capital, Ford Motor Credit, IBM Credit,
and GMAC at the end of 1990 was less than 10 percent. Ignoring reserves against loan losses, which were not reported, these ratios would
not have been sufficient for them to meet the tier 1 plus tier 2 test
for a "well-capitalized" bank established by the regulators this year.
Moreover, over this period finance companies were able to raise their
leverage ratios without a corresponding downgrade in credit ratings,
and thus they were able to operate at marginal capital ratios not far
from those of banks—11.6 percent was the average for fast-growing
companies, while some operated with significantly lower marginal
ratios.

In fact, the study concluded that the marginal cost of funds for banks
and finance companies was about the same. Finance companies operated with somewhat higher marginal capital ratios than banks, but that
was largely offset by the fact that they had access to relatively cheap
equity capital from their diversified parent organizations, an advantage denied to bank holding companies.[7] The rates they had to pay on
commercial paper were about the same as what banks had to pay for
large Cds. Finance companies would have to pay commitment fees for
backup credit lines and placement fees, but banks would have to pay
deposit insurance premiums and the opportunity cost of required reserves. Bottom line, the authors estimated that finance companies had
about a 10-basis-point cost of funds advantage.

The study was pre-FDICIA, over a period when banks were paying
8 basis points for deposit insurance. In the post-FDICIA environment,

capital ratios will be equalized, and banks will be paying from 23 to 31 basis points for domestic deposits (although reserve requirements have been reduced). The study also ignored the cost of regulation, which is going up as a result of FDICIA. A recent study by the American Bankers Association estimated that the direct cost of regulatory compliance exclusive of deposit insurance premiums, examination fees, and foregone interest on reserves amounted to $10.7 billion a year. FDICIA is expected to bring the regulatory burden tab up to $15 billion. The official report on regulatory burdens by the Federal Financial Institutions Examination Council (FFIEC), released on December 17, estimates that the annual cost of regulatory compliance may be as high as $17.5 billion. I am not aware of any way to determine what proportion of these costs is fixed versus variable, and so I do not know precisely how it will affect the marginal cost of funds comparison for banks and finance companies. But $17.5 billion a year on an asset base of $3.5 trillion amounts to an average regulatory cost burden per dollar of assets of 50 basis points. Considering the effects of higher deposit insurance premiums, higher capital requirements, and an add factor for regulatory burdens, a reasonable guess is that, at the margin, finance companies will have about a 50–70 basis point funding advantage over commercial banks.

PREDICTIONS

In closing let me offer a few predictions.

—The strong profits reported by the banking industry in 1992, largely the result of a favorable interest rate environment and an improving economy, are masking a secular deterioration in prospects for banking as a result of the cumulative impact of rising bank regulatory burdens. The banking sector will continue to shrink relative to the economy and to overall financial flows. The rising cost and declining volume of depository intermediation will have a depressing effect on real activity in the short run and a resource allocation effect in the longer run. Those without direct or indirect access to the securities markets, will be the most directly affected. Because this outcome is at least in part an artifact of the regulatory system, this means further reliance of forms of finance that are intrinsically less efficient than banking.

—Finance companies, and perhaps also foreign banks, will continue to grow and take up the slack in the middle market lending business. Business loan sale and asset securitization programs will also develop rapidly with a great deal of experimentation involving overcollateralization, senior or subordinated structures, third-party guarantees, and other types of credit enhancements. The junk bond market, which began a resurgence in 1992, will continue to blossom. However, all of this will take time. We are in for a protracted period during which small to mid-sized companies will have difficulty obtaining credit.

—Reflecting the high fixed cost component to regulatory compliance, the number of banking organizations will shrink at an accelerating pace. It is exceedingly expensive and difficult for any banking organization to understand and to develop the necessary compliance procedures for all of the new rules coming on stream. Smaller banks will have the hardest time, however, and many of them will be inclined to seek a solution via merger.

—At least some banks that vigorously opposed the core bank-wholesale bank model espoused by Robert Litan and others will begin to lobby for this approach as an optional structure in order to contain their exposure to regulatory burdens.

NOTES

1. In their paper in this volume, George G. Kaufman and George J. Benston refer to these as structured early intervention and resolution.
2. In the end, several money center banks joined independent bankers in opposing amendments that would have permitted interstate banking in exchange for rollbacks of bank insurance and securities powers.
3. As is often the case with consumer regulations, many of these provisions will have perverse effects for consumers. For a good analysis, see "The Burden of Bank Regulation: Tracing the Costs Imposed by Bank Regulation on the American Public," paper prepared for the American Bankers Association by the Secura Group, November 16, 1992.
4. Joshua Feinman and Richard Porter, "The Continuing Weakness in M2," Finance and Economics Discussion Series Paper 209 (Federal Reserve Board, September 1992).
5. Herbert Baer and John McElravey, "Capital Adequacy and the Growth of U.S. Banks," Working Paper Series WP-92-11 (Federal Reserve Bank of Chicago, June 1992).
6. Eli Remolona and Kurt Wulfekuhler, "Finance Companies, Bank Competi-

tion, and Niche Markets," *Federal Reserve Bank of New York Quarterly Review,* Summer 1992.

7. Of the twenty largest finance companies, twelve are wholly owned subsidiaries of nonfinancial firms such as General Electric, three are owned by nonbank financial parents, three are affiliated with banks, and two are independent.

Implementation of the Act: Key Regulations and Regulatory Proposals

KAREN D. SHAW

FDICIA at One: A Troublesome Toddler at Best

Engineers like to say that God is in the details. For bankers, the devil may be in the details, at least as far as FDICIA is concerned.

When the FDIC Improvement Act was being debated by Congress, few in the industry recognized the sweeping redefinition of the regulatory landscape that would result. Beguiled by talk of interstate branching and new powers, many bankers realized the statute's full impact only as its implementing regulations became effective. Even as the industry tries to reverse some of the provisions to which it takes the greatest exception, it is still forced to come to terms with the law as it is and will be.

This panel has been asked to focus on four specific elements of the law: prompt, corrective action; deposit insurance; interest rate risk-based capital; and real estate lending guidelines. This is an interesting, if diverse, list, since it includes cornerstones of the new law that are unlikely to be revised by any imminent legislative initiatives. As a result, FDICIA's changes in these areas should be viewed as fundamental new elements in any financial institution's strategic plan.

PROMPT, CORRECTIVE ACTION

Section 131 of FDICIA requires the regulators to institute immediate and remedial responses to any insured depository that falls below stated capital standards. In many ways, this section should be viewed as the cornerstone of the act as a whole. It spells out the capital-based regulatory standards on which the Treasury premised its initial legislative recommendations, and on which Congress subsequently acted.

The law required the agencies to have the Section 131 rules in place and in effect by December 19, 1992. Thus we know already what the statutory standards will mean in practice and how the implementing regulations should be revised.

First, of course, the standards were to create the "December surprise"—or December fizzle, as it proved. Far fewer institutions than anticipated fall below the Section 131 "critical capital" threshold, partly because the FDIC has closed some troubled banks and partly because the industry has improved its capitalization through months of record earnings. Some last minute fiddling by the Office of Thrift Supervision (OTS) with thrift capital standards has also taken the bang out of the surprise.

While the agencies had no discretion over where to set the critical capital threshold, the law did not define the "well-capitalized" and "adequately capitalized" standards to which many other provisions in FDICIA are tied. Here the agencies seem to have gone a bit overboard in their initial implementing rules. They set a very high test for well-capitalized, especially in the tier 1 and leverage standards. While these higher standards may ultimately be well justified, they seem excessive in the current recessionary environment. If one sought to encourage new extensions of credit, one might choose to phase in tough new capital standards, giving banks and thrifts time to raise capital while they also promote the nation's needed economic recovery.

One of the initial criticisms of the prompt, corrective action provisions in FDICIA is their blunt instrument quality. The General Accounting Office and many others pointed out that capital is a most unreliable indicator of bank condition. As a result, the statute allowed regulators to include other factors in their application of the Section 131 sanctions. The implementing rules permit regulators to downgrade an institution one capital rung if other supervisory issues raise concern. However, the agencies did not choose to raise institutions one notch if other factors warranted a positive view of the bank. Using Section 131 only to punish institutions seems not only overcautious, but also counterproductive.

Institutions should be rewarded for good risk management and for other practices that regulators seek to encourage—and the Section 131 standards are the ideal vehicle to begin this incentive-oriented approach to bank regulation.

DEPOSIT INSURANCE

On December 15, 1992, the FDIC put into place its new system of risk-based deposit insurance premiums. In doing so, however, the agency asked questions that make clear that this permanent schedule will be but a passing phase. Significant revisions will be made before a final, truly permanent system of risk-based deposit insurance premiums is instituted.

One of the biggest problems the FDIC has had is determining just what risks cause losses to the deposit insurance fund. As noted above, capital is a very poor indicator of bank safety. Many of the large Texas banks, for example, were well-capitalized the day they failed. Thus, racheting premiums to capital would be inaccurate and, probably, counterproductive. Adding the other factors that go into the capital adequacy, asset quality, management, earnings, liquidity (CAMEL) rating would be appropriate, if an institution's CAMEL was not supposed to be a deep, dark secret. As a result, the FDIC developed a composite risk-based structure that reflects both the capital and CAMEL ratings, but also includes other "black-box" factors the FDIC may choose to consider.

The law actually gives the FDIC broad authority to bear in mind more than these supervisory issues. The agency can, for example, vary the risk-based premium according to the size of an institution, presumably to reflect any "too-big-to-fail" type of risk. It can also vary premiums according to the amount of uninsured liabilities an institution assumes, again reflecting concern that the agency might not be able to avoid covering a big bank in whole during an emergency.

Thus any changes the agency might choose to make later in the risk-based premium structure could say a lot about how it will handle troubled banks in the future. Should the FDIC decide to put in place a proxy premium against uninsured deposits through the risk-based schedule, for example, this would signal a continuation of Reagan and Bush administration policies of protecting virtually all depositors all the time. Clearly, Congress did not intend this. It included in FDICIA a meaningful least-cost test, designed to force the FDIC to liquidate troubled banks without paying off uninsured depositors unless another alternative was genuinely cheaper.

Although FDICIA included many significant changes to deposit insurance, one important reform was omitted from the final law. Treasury had recommended that deposit insurance coverage be limited to no more than $100,000 per individual per institution. Many small banks vigorously opposed this change, believing that funds would flee to banks thought too big to fail. As a result, the limit on multiple coverage was deleted early in the legislative debate.

This was a very serious omission from the final law. As long as the government chooses to subsidize risky institutions by protecting deposits well in excess of the average amounts placed by the average retail customer, the banking industry will be hard-pressed to argue either for regulatory relief or for sweeping structural change. When the government is on the hook for virtually all the liabilities of an insured institution, it has a natural interest in governing that institution's activities.

Small banks should take heart from the changes in FDICIA regarding the least-cost test and the new risk-based premium. They also ought not to neglect the substantive changes in recent FDIC policy regarding failing banks. In 1992, the FDIC allowed uninsured depositors to take losses, even when very good-sized institutions, like First City, were closed. If the industry genuinely wants to get the government off its back—or at least out of its boardroom—it must come to terms with limits on deposit insurance.

INTEREST-RATE RISK-BASED CAPITAL

Section 305 of FDICIA requires regulators to put in place by June 19, 1993, three significant revisions to the current risk-based capital standard. The first of these is an interest-rate risk component. With an advance notice of proposed rulemaking already before the industry on this aspect of capital, the implications of this change can be seen clearly.

The current risk-based capital system is being blamed by many in the industry, and on Capitol Hill, for causing the so-called credit crunch. These critics point to the 100-percent risk-weighting for commercial loans and contrast this with the zero-percent risk weight for government securities. Clearly this is an inducement to move a portfolio into governments, especially at a time when the tight new capital sanctions required by Section 131 are being implemented. Since government securities do, in fact, carry an interest-rate risk, changing the capital standard to reflect this is one way to address the credit-crunch worry without instituting broad capital forbearance or using the capital standards more explicitly to allocate credit.

As a result, the Clinton administration should be expected to move aggressively to institute interest-rate risk-based capital in compliance with the FDICIA mandate. This is one area where the administration can move without raising concerns about regulatory laxity—avoiding harsh criticism from Representative Henry Gonzalez or others on the Hill. It is also a meaningful response to the credit availability problem, because the distortions in the current risk-based capital standards clearly have had an effect on portfolio decisions in recent months.

However, the administration will face a broader challenge as it considers the new capital standards. As noted above, Section 305 adds three capital standards, not just interest-rate risk. The other two requirements of the act are capital based on "asset concentration" and the risk of "nontraditional" activities. These latter two standards are far more difficult to define than interest-rate risk, and even a quick look at the advance notice of proposed rulemaking (ANPR) on interest-rate risk will show how hard that was.

The industry ignores the implementation of concentration and activity risk-based capital at its very great peril. Defining concentration, especially for community banks, is a tricky business. The old know-your-customer rule of banking inevitably resulted in concentrated portfolios. Similarly, institutions that developed special areas of lending expertise naturally also had concentrated portfolios. It is easy to spot risky concentrations in retrospect, as the ill effects of an overemphasis on real estate or less developed countries (LDCs) become clear, but it is far harder to anticipate areas of risk and reflect them meaningfully in concentration standards.

The nontraditional activity risk-based component is even more problematic. Many nontraditional activities are far safer than the old-style lending that got banks and thrifts in trouble. Diversifying income streams is essential to improving bank profitability, which, in turn, is the only reliable way to reduce potential risk to the deposit insurance funds. It is also critical to developing a competitive, efficient financial system. Thus implementing the FDICIA requirement for a new capital component in this area should be undertaken only with great care, and thought should be given to eliminating—by statute—this difficult, and perhaps counterproductive, requirement.

REAL ESTATE LENDING GUIDELINES

The controversy over the loan-to-value (LTV) rules implementing Section 304 epitomizes the confusion in the debate over the law. Initially, Section 304 required the agencies to implement specific LTVs for different types of real estate loans. This was not, as some suggest, a dastardly plot dreamed up by a Congress bent on micromanaging the industry. It came instead from the FDIC. Responding to concerns raised by both financial institutions and the real estate industry, Congress toned down the agency's original proposal, allowing regulators to institute broad standards, instead of specific mandatory LTVs.

However, when the agencies came to propose their LTV rules, there was much huffing and puffing about Congress. Complaining about the amount of detail in the law's requirements, the agencies proposed the specific LTVs that had been in the original FDIC legislative draft. Only after another round of vigorous industry protest did the agencies agree on "guidelines" that do not specifically mandate LTVs. This should be viewed as a major victory for reasonableness in regulation.

Implementing FDICIA — An Interim Assessment

Since its enactment by Congress at the end of 1991, the FDIC Improvement Act has not had very good press. The banking industry roundly criticized the act, and the American Bankers Association launched a campaign to achieve a list of twenty changes in the banking laws.[1] William Isaac, a regulator turned banking consultant, now leading the campaign of the Secura Group against the act, called for the repeal of FDICIA "in its entirety." And the principal regulatory authorities have not been much kinder. Federal Reserve Governor LaWare characterized the act as containing "enough Mickey Mouse provisions to make Disney sue for patent infringement."[2] Treasury Secretary Brady called it "regulatory overkill."[3] And President Bush himself described FDICIA as "the highest expression of the over-regulatory mindset."[4]

More specifically, critics allege that the act plunges regulators into the micromanagement of banking institutions and creates a regulatory burden so heavy that banks may be rendered noncompetitive. The new capital requirements are seen as leading to a credit crunch. And the epitome of foolishness is alleged to have been reached in a provision requiring the banking agencies to set a standard for the minimum ratio of market to book value for the stock of publicly held banks or holding companies—does Congress think the agencies can regulate stock market prices?

Against these criticisms, of course, should be weighed the objectives of the legislation, which do not seem to get equal emphasis in the discussion. In broad terms, FDICIA can be seen as an attempt to correct the perverse incentives of two groups, bank management and banking agency management, which contributed so greatly to the financial disasters of the 1980s.[5] As to bank management, the act undertakes in a number of ways to reduce the moral hazard problem that is now widely recognized as having been a fatal design flaw in our deposit insurance system.[6] In particular, the act calls for a structure of higher capital requirements more promptly enforced, for cutting back sharply on the use of too-big-to-fail approaches to handling bank failures and protecting uninsured claimants, and for the introduction of a system of risk-based deposit insurance premium assessments.

As to agency management, the strategy of the act is to try to counteract the tendency toward forbearance in enforcement and closure that was so much in evidence and so costly throughout the 1980s.[7] The main techniques for achieving that objective are to call for improved accounting disclosure of an institution's current economic condition and to reduce the agency's scope of discretion under the statute and thus its freedom not to take action. Ultimately, however, Congress still placed reliance on the agencies, especially the FDIC, to define and implement the provisions of the act by regulation and to exercise their augmented powers in individual cases.

In making this first anniversary assessment of agency performance in implementing FDICIA, we are looking at a process by no means completed. On some provisions we have final rules, but on most we have only proposed regulations or preliminary announcements or nothing at all. It should also be noted that FDICIA is a lengthy enactment—167 pages, in the House Conference Report form. It would take all day to go through the act section by section. Therefore, I am constrained to singling out a few sections that are pertinent to both the objectives and the criticisms of the act. In evaluating their implementation, I will focus on two criteria: (1) Does the action taken further—or impede—the legislative goal of establishing a framework that will effect the desired changes in the behavior of agency management and bank management?; and (2) have the regulations been drafted in a way that increases or diminishes the grounds for criticism?

SECTION 131

FDICIA Section 131, on prompt corrective action for capital deficiencies (new FDIA Section 38), is of central importance in its own right and also one of the relatively few statutes for which we have the final rule.[8] It set up a structure of at least two capital ratios and five capital categories, but left it to the agencies to define the capital ratios and set the minimum levels for each category. The rule adopts the three capital

TABLE 1. *Definition of Capital Categories*
Percent

Category		Tier 1 capital ratio		Total capital ratio		Leverage ratio
Well capitalized	≥	6	and	10	and	5
Adequately capitalized	≥	4	and	8	and	4
Undercapitalized	≥	3	and	6	and	3
Significantly undercapitalized	<	3	or	6	or	3
Critically undercapitalized	≤		2% tangible equity to total assets			

ratios that were already in use: the ratio of tier 1 (or core) capital to risk-weighted total assets, the ratio of total capital to risk-weighted total assets, and the ratio of tier 1 capital to total assets without any risk-weighting discounts (the leverage ratio). The rule also set the minimum level (to be "adequately capitalized") for each ratio at the same number as previously in effect and then distributed the other categories as shown in table 1.

How are these ratios and levels to be judged by our criteria? There are certainly shortcomings in the four-category scheme of risk-weightings (really risk-discountings) that go into the calculation of the first two ratios, and one can criticize the tier 1 capital definition as well.[9] But these derive from the earlier implementation of the Basle Accord of 1988, not FDICIA.

The levels are another matter. There is no increase in the required minimum ratios for adequate capitalization over those already in effect. The new category of "critically undercapitalized," which is intended to set in motion a process of speedy sale or closure for institutions probably already economically insolvent, was set at the lowest figure permitted by the statute. The rule does not reflect any continuing push toward higher capital on the agencies' part.

Furthermore, one can ask where the assigned levels, new or old, come from. In theory, one could estimate the asset portfolio volatility of a bank and derive a capital level that would make a given deposit insurance premium adequate to cover losses within some confidence interval.[10] It is difficult to avoid the impression, however, that the num-

TABLE 2. *Classification of U.S. Banks by Capital Categories*

Category and quarter[a]	Number of banks	Assets (billions of dollars)	Tier 1 capital ratio	Total capital ratio	Leverage ratio
Well capitalized					
92.2	10,909	2,229.7	11.5	13.4	7.7
92.3	10,931	2,688.2	10.7	13.0	7.7
Adequately capitalized					
92.2	514	1,124.7	6.3	9.1	5.6
92.3	443	724.7	6.3	9.0	5.5
Undercapitalized					
92.2	139	45.5	5.6	7.3	4.5
92.3	106	31.8	5.8	7.4	4.3
Significantly under- capitalized					
92.2	49	10.2	4.1	5.4	2.9
92.3	46	7.9	3.8	5.2	3.1
Critically under- capitalized					
92.2	46	7.8	1.5	2.7	1.1
92.3	36	7.3	0.5	1.3	0.3

Source: Federal Reserve Bank of Dallas.
[a]Third quarter data are preliminary.

bers adopted have little to do with theoretical adequacy and much to do with political pragmatics. It is no doubt reassuring to learn that by these standards 98.5 percent of U.S. banks are well or adequately capitalized, and a mere three-tenths of 1 percent are critically under-capitalized. The 1992 data are given in table 2.

The second noteworthy aspect of FDICIA Section 131 is the rather innovative way in which it attempts to narrow agency enforcement discretion and press for prompter intervention. The statute establishes a structure of mandatory, presumptive, and discretionary corrective actions, geared to declining capital categories, that the banking agencies are supposed to utilize. It is an ingenious idea, but it has its practical limitations.

The statute prescribes four steps that the agency must take with regard to any undercapitalized institution: monitor it closely, require an acceptable capital restoration plan, permit only approved asset growth, and require approval for any expansion of offices or lines of business. The mandatory nature of these actions is more procedural than substantive, since in the final analysis each comes back to the agency's own determination of what is appropriate.

For significantly undercapitalized institutions, the statute specifies some presumptive corrective measures. That is, the agency must require recapitalization through sale of stock or merger, restrict affiliate transactions, and restrict deposit interest rates to prevailing levels— unless the agency determines that such an action would not be helpful. And for each category of undercapitalization, there is an additional list of explicitly discretionary enforcement steps that the agency may take.

The implementing regulations under Section 38 mainly address procedures for the time of determination of capital categories and for issuing and responding to directives to take corrective actions. As for the corrective actions themselves, the regulations simply echo the provisions and structure of the statute. The overall thrust of the statute is clear enough: corrective supervisory response to undercapitalization is necessary and normal, and the burden of justification in the event of inaction is on the agency. It would seem appropriate, therefore, to require the agency to document the reasons for not acting, but the statute does not explicitly so demand, nor does the regulation. The agencies' attitude toward this effort to change their behavior away from forbearance will become clear only as they accumulate a record of applying their statutory powers to undercapitalized banks.

What about the applicability of the types of criticisms of FDICIA mentioned earlier? How seriously one ought to take the credit crunch line of argument depends critically on the definition and demonstration of the existence of a credit crunch, issues beyond the scope of this paper. But it is certainly true that the risk-weighting formula employed in two of the capital ratios makes investing in commercial loans more capital-costly to a bank than investing in government securities. More generally, any risk-weighting process will affect asset choices—as it is intended to. The real issue is how close to getting it right the Basle Accord does come. Without recognition of interest rate risk and concentration risk, the answer is definitely that it does not come very close. But the moral of this story is to improve the Basle formula, as I hope is slowly being accomplished. It is not primarily a FDICIA matter, although the June 1993 deadline of Section 305 may help speed the process.

The other favorite criticism of FDICIA is that it inflicts supervisory micromanagement upon banks. For the bottom two capital categories, that is just about accurate. FDIC is given a wide array of controls over bank operation and management personnel, and is definitely expected to use them. On the other hand, there is a high probability that banks in those categories are already insolvent, or next to insolvent, in economic terms. FDIC had better be essentially running such banks, unless you would like to see a rerun of the S&L debacle. For well-capitalized or even adequately capitalized banks, there are few additional constraints imposed by this part of FDICIA. So the fear expressed by banks of micromanagement under Section 38 constitutes an added reason to continue to meet its rather modest capital standards, and that is probably a constructive incentive.

SECTION 132

The next provision I wish to examine, about which much anxiety has been expressed, is Section 132 (new FDIA Section 39) calling for promulgation of safety and soundness standards, dealing with such subjects as asset quality, internal controls, loan documentation, credit underwriting, interest rate exposure, asset growth, and compensation. At this time, all that the agencies have issued is a preliminary notice of proposed rulemaking, which recites the statute and asks a series of questions.[11]

According to the release, the "overriding issue" in implementing the section is how to balance the statutory objectives against the need to avoid establishing unrealistic and overly burdensome standards that unnecessarily raise costs. Therefore, the agencies state that they intend to prescribe, not "inflexible standards specifying how depository institutions must be managed," but "standards designed to prevent institutions from developing serious problems." Commenters are invited to provide specific language for this purpose.

As framed, the task seems impossible to accomplish. General standards, leaving management operating flexibility, are unlikely to be able to "prevent institutions from developing serious problems."[12] By definition, standards are somewhat broad and imprecise, dependent in their administration upon a further exercise of judgment.[13] They are not bright-line rules, intended to be more objectively defined and self-executing—like the capital ratios under Section 138. The distinction between standards and rules is, to lawyers, a basic one. Congress should be presumed to have made the reference to "standards" in Section 39, and not elsewhere, with knowledge of the difference.

Therefore, contrary to the implication of many of the questions in the preliminary notice, the objective of agency implementation should not be to turn the statute into a set of specific requirements or limits on bank management in each of the subject areas. Indeed, I would suggest that the agencies hark back to the point made at the outset of this paper—that the act has two main goals: to define and bound agency discretion as well as affect the behavior of bank management. Both would be served if the standards were defined by circumstances that would cause the agency to initiate an inquiry into the possible necessity of a corrective plan or to use others of its now vast array of powers.

In other words, the standards are not cast by the statute as a set of commands to bank management and do not have to be reformulated in such terms by the agencies. Nor do the agencies have to attempt to think of every relevant factor that might enter into a judgment in each of these broad domains of bank operation, as would be required for a fully specified rule. Instead, they should think in terms of formulating published guidelines as to the conditions or states of affairs that would trigger further agency investigation and consideration of the need for possible enforcement action. Bank management would be on notice and able to conduct its affairs accordingly.

Here is a specific example of the difference in approach I am suggesting, for probably the most often derided provision in the act. Section 39(b)(1)(C) calls on the banking agencies to prescribe standards specifying, to the extent feasible, a minimum ratio of market value to book value for publicly traded shares of banks or bank holding companies. The reaction of a Secura Group executive is typical: the provision is "particularly troublesome," because "management has no control over its market to book value ratio."[14] The comment is followed by a reference to factors that cause market prices to fluctuate.

Viewed as a command to control the market price of a bank's stock, the section would indeed be troubling. But of course that is not what it says. It deals with the ratio of market to book value, and calls for setting a minimum standard, such as, for example, 0.8. Why would the market value of net assets fall below their book value? Certainly one possibility is that the book value reflects some asset acquisition costs that are now far above their current worth. In other words, the ratio can give a signal that the financial statement book values, including the book value of capital, may be misleading and should not be relied on.

So when the stock's market-to-book ratio falls substantially below 1, there can be good reason to take a closer look at those accounting numbers and the need for adjustment in asset carrying values. Viewed not as a command but as a published guideline as to when the agency would inaugurate such an inquiry, the minimum ratio standard called for by the statute makes perfectly good sense.

SECTION 112

Consideration of the reliability of accounting statements brings me to the final provisions I wish to examine, FDICIA Section 112 (new Section 36) and Section 121 (new Section 37) dealing with accounting reforms and improved auditing and financial reporting. These are vital matters, for the whole structure of capital requirements is no better than the accounting numbers on which it is calculated. Positive net worth based on irrelevant paper values has characterized many of the S&L and bank failures of the last decade.[15]

Section 36 established somewhat stricter auditing requirements and invited FDIC to expand the scope of financial disclosure and extend the accountants' review to quarterly as well as annual financial reports. Judging from the rule proposed to implement Section 36, FDIC intends to decline that invitation.[16] The proposed rule, in accordance with the statute, does require auditors to attest to new statements by management in its annual report about the effectiveness of internal controls and compliance with a specifically designated set of laws and regulations (covering affiliate transactions, lending limits, insider loans, dividend restrictions, and call reports).

But when it comes to financial statement disclosure, FDIC apparently intends to stay with present Generally Accepted Accounting Principles (GAAP) rules and annual audits. Section 37 called on the banking agencies to review their accounting procedures and principles so that bank reports shall accurately reflect their capital, and to develop "a method . . . to provide supplemental disclosure of the estimated fair market value of assets and liabilities, to the extent feasible and practicable, in any balance sheet, financial statement, report of condition, or other report." No major release reporting on that review has been issued, and I understand none is to be expected.

Thus the implementation of Section 36 and Section 37 calls for more emphasis on regulatory compliance but not on market value disclosure. The banking agencies have consistently displayed unbroken hostility to, not only market value accounting, but even market value footnote disclosure. Congress invited, but did not compel, them to reconsider their stance in light of the experience of the 1980s and the new reliance on capital requirements. But any changes in this area will clearly have to come from the Financial Accounting Standards Board, pressed by the SEC but opposed by the banking industry and its agencies.

CONCLUSION

What conclusions can we draw, based on and limited to this particular set of FDICIA provisions? So much is yet to come that any analysis is provisional, but some tendencies seem clear.

First, as to furthering the purposes of the act, the agencies seem to be following a minimalist strategy—they will go as far as the act forces them, but no further. In particular, they evidence little sympathy with those aspects of the law intended to reduce their own discretion.

That, I would suggest, should give taxpayers some reason for concern. After all, the political pressures that led to constant forbearance over the last decade are not all that much different today, though the public may, for the moment, have a dim awareness of how much they cost.

If, for example, the stringency or leniency of capital requirements depends critically on supervisory decisions on whether or not to order asset writedowns, the objectivity of the capital categories is somewhat illusory. Market value accounting or disclosure, however partially implemented, would take away some of that discretion—which is one reason it remains so highly unpopular with the agencies as well as the industry.

Second, how good a job have the agencies been doing of avoiding unnecessary costs? The answer is still unclear. Much depends on how, for instance, Section 39 on safety and soundness standards is finally implemented, and we do not yet have even a proposed rule. However the general tone of the advance notice release is not especially encouraging.

NOTES

1. "Financial Institutions, ABA, State Bankers Identify 20 Statute Provisions to Repeal or Modify," *BNA Daily Report for Executives*, April 30, 1992, p. A-17.

2. "FED's LaWare Predicts Ultimate Repeal of Most Onerous Parts of FIRREA, FDICIA," *BNA Banking Report*, June 22, 1992, p. 1090. The governor is not too clear on the distinction between patent and copyright laws.

3. "Bill Calls for Easing of Regulations on Banks," United Press International, June 24, 1992.

4. "What the Candidates Pledge To Do for Banking," *American Banker*, October 19, 1992, p. 13.

5. For a more detailed exposition, see the excellent paper by Richard S. Carnell, "A Partial Antidote to Perverse Incentives: The FDIC Improvement Act of 1991," *Annual Review of Banking Law*, vol. 12 (1993), pp. 317–71.

6. See, for example, Kenneth Scott, "The Moral Hazard Hypothesis," in Richard J. Herring and Ashish C. Shah, eds., *Reforming the American Banking System* (Wharton Financial Institution Center, 1991), p. 1.

7. See, for example, Edward Kane, "Taxpayer Losses in Deposit Insurance: The Incentive-Conflict Hypothesis," in Herring and Shah, *Reforming the American Banking System*.

8. 57 Fed. Reg. 44866, September 29, 1992.

9. See Shadow Financial Regulatory Committee, Statements 6, 18, 19, 29, and 44, *Journal of Financial Services Research*, vol. 6, supplement (August 1992).

10. R. Merton, "An Analytic Derivation of the Cost of Deposit Insurance and Loan Guarantees," *Journal of Banking and Finance*, vol. 1 (June 1977), p. 3.

11. 57 Fed. Reg. 31336, July 15, 1992.

12. The seriousness of a problem depends greatly on the capacity of the institution to absorb any associated losses, so we are brought back to the issues of capital measurement and capital levels. The Section 39 standards have to be seen in light of the Section 38 categories.

13. Compare P. Schlag, "Rules and Standards," *UCLA Law Review*, vol. 33, no. 2 (1985), p. 379.

14. R. Bubel, "FDICIA Imposes Increased Responsibilities on Bank and Thrift Managements," *Banking Policy Report*, vol. 11 (October 5, 1992), p. 1.

15. See D. Toumey, "Bank Regulation, Bank Accounting and Bank Failures," *1991 Annual Survey of American Law* (New York University School of Law, 1992), pp. 823, 843 (table of 12 most costly resolutions).

16. 57 Fed. Reg. 42516, September 15, 1992.

EDWARD J. KANE

Comments

Since Bill Clinton became president-elect, we have heard a great deal about FOBs: Friends of Bill. Job files for FOBs are each said to carry a number that inversely orders the strength of the friendship. On the ordering used, the future first lady would be FOB1. This, of course, is the reverse of the ordering that would obtain in the British royal family. Focusing on enmity rather than friendship, I have been developing a file on FOFs: Foes of FDICIA. So far, the lowest numbers in my file have been won by a few Federal Reserve and Treasury officials, with some miscreant exregulators and banking trade association spokespersons close behind.

In my experience, it is spoiled children who complain the loudest about parental discipline. For taxpayers, "Skeptics of the Bill" would probably make a more telling acronym. Administrators' objections to FDICIA's curtailing of their discretion to forbear are logically fallacious. They ask us to let good possibilities outweigh bad probabilities. They emphasize the good ways agency officials could use the lost discretion, while refusing to acknowledge the temptations that have repeatedly led them and their predecessors to abuse this discretion.

At this very moment, officials are pushing the bank insurance fund (BIF) into the same ruts in the same road that FSLIC took in 1983. Their continued willingness to help put off bank asset writedowns and to delay the resolution of economically insolvent deposit institutions places a poor bet for taxpayers, a bet that is nevertheless welcomed by the weakest and loudest segment of the industry. At the same time it should be recognized that trade association lobbying positions are apt to be biased in favor of weak institutions. This is because a financial industry's weakest members can and do earn profits from building up a disproportionate and life-sustaining degree of clout in industry trade associations.

Because delay is costly, it breaks faith with other taxpayers and with the spirit of the FDIC Improvement Act of 1991 (FDICIA). The central thrust of the 1991 legislation is to insist that, when, and as, an insured institution's capital position declines, its managers are confronted with a mandate to recapitalize their firm promptly or else. The virtue of this exit-policy mandate is that it subjects a weakening firm to the same sort of discipline that its creditors would impose if they weren't insured against loss by the FDIC. It is important to understand that recapitalization does not imply the disappearance of a bank's assets nor even of its franchise. What it does imply is a timely repricing of bank assets and a market testing of the value of keeping a troubled institution in play.

Identifying timely demands for recapitalization as regulatory excess that dictates a mindless shrinking of the banking industry is part of a nasty public-relations campaign that bank trade associations and some federal regulators are waging against the FDIC Improvement Act of 1991. This campaign uses all three of the nonpecuniary tools of the unprincipled special-interest lobbyist. These tools are mischaracterization, distortion, and exaggeration. The campaign mischaracterizes transitional costs from changing regulatory patterns as if they were permanent burdens. In addition, it exaggerates FDICIA's curtailment of regulatory discretion as far more restrictive than it truly is. It distorts the extent to which recapitalization pressure is apt to aggravate the nation's financial problems by alleging that it will worsen an already waning, transitional shortage of credit and put destructive pressure on weak institutions.

The central purpose of FDICIA is to inhibit the doubling and redoubling of deposit-institution losses that have already occurred. The campaign ignores survey evidence that indicates that a substantial majority of ordinary bankers support this regulatory principle and other regulatory strategies embodied in FDICIA. The SOBs or FOFs (Foes of FDICIA) characterize the idea of restricting regulators' discretion not as a strategy for protecting strong institutions and unwary taxpayers from gambling by weak institutions, but as a recipe for whipping up actuarially avoidable losses in weak institutions.

Accounting loopholes make the economic value of bank capital hard to observe. As long as lobbyists can hold market-value accounting at bay, the tripwire system of capital discipline needs to be supplemented with secondary triggers able to provide timely signals of a hidden worsening in an insured institution's enterprise-contributed net worth. Parallels exist between the detailed regulatory standards the act requires regulators to develop and covenants in private contracts that convey renegotiation rights in situations where changes in a borrower's condition are hard to observe and can occur suddenly. Recognizing this parallel clarifies that regulators' have an *obligation* to waive covenant violations when close investigation shows the violations to be inconsequential. Nevertheless, the call for standards is being depicted as a completely misguided strategy of regulatory micromanagement. I heard one regulator characterize the FDIC Improvement Act on my campus in October 1992 as an "oxymoron of the first order," full of "asinine provisions" that request regulatory standards that no one needs. One week earlier, Treasury Secretary Nicholas Brady opined to conferees at the annual meeting of the American Bankers Association that the burden of regulatory compliance "had reached a level that is intolerable" and called for reestablishing "a balanced approach to lending and risk-taking." One wonders whether, by a "balanced approach," he means the approach FSLIC managed to promote.

By and large, federal regulators are carrying out their responsibilities under the act in an unfriendly spirit. I will cite two examples of this.

First, FDICIA requires that regulators incorporate interest-rate risk into the risk-based capital regulatory framework. Interest-rate risk refers to the danger that future movements in market interest rates will induce a net adverse revaluation of the asset and liability positions an institution holds. In response to the FDICIA requirement, federal bank regulators issued in July a proposed rule that fails to develop either an effective measure of a bank's exposure to interest-rate risk or an effective framework for limiting the extent to which these exposures pass through to the net reserves of the BIF.[1] Although easy-to-use computer software for interest-rate risk analysis is in use at many banks and available from private vendors such as Fiserv, the proposal emphasizes pencil-and-paper simplicity in reporting requirements. It seeks to estimate what would happen to the net value of an institution's on- and off-balance-sheet positions if interest rates moved 100 basis points in either direction. To this end, it assigns each position an "approximate" price-volatility risk weight established by the banking agencies. Finally, the agencies plan to use the resulting measures only to identify and discipline banks that are taking high levels of interest-rate risk relative to their peers.

Given the billions of dollars at stake and the availability of modern information technology, it is outrageous to let simplicity in reporting procedures outweigh the need for banks and regulators to examine how a bank's true exposure to the range of likely interest-rate changes affects its capital (which occurs by raising the required rate of return to equity investors) and to calculate the value of the loss exposure interest-rate risk imposes on the BIF. Because interest rates tend to rise and fall in cyclical fashion, potential upward and downward swings in prospective interest rates seldom appear symmetric. Although short-term and long-term rates tend to move in the same direction, swings in these rates do not tend to affect asset and liability value equally. Near the start of a recovery in particular, the range of possible interest-rate increases far exceeds the range of probable decreases, and nasty declines in long-term asset values can occur with great suddenness.

Worst of all, the proposal makes no effort to incorporate the cumulative interaction of past interest-rate risk taking and actual interest-rate movements into the capital ratio that triggers FDICIA's tripwire system of regulatory discipline. Given the damage interest-rate risk did to FSLIC, it is a disgrace that authorities have not installed an adequate system for measuring interest-rate risk by now. If such a system were in place, it would clarify the urgency of recapitalizing a number of seriously distressed banks as soon as possible. Today some of these banks are blithely telling us that their bet is okay because long rates are going to fall this year even if short rates rise.[2]

The proposed regulatory structure for measuring and controlling interest-rate risk mandated under FDICIA illustrates the growing conflict developing between the chairmen of the congressional banking committees and top federal banking regulators. This tension reinforces the theory that regulatory forbearance aggravated the FSLIC mess and is underscored by these parties' respective attitudes toward coming clean about the size of the shortage in the BIF's explicit reserves. Consider the contrast between two statements made in March 1991 as comments on the sizable adjustments then being made in FDIC loss estimates for the bank insurance fund.

Chairman of the House Banking Committee Henry Gonzalez: "We must avoid a rerun of the shifting numbers, the gimmickry, and the outright deceit that marked so much of the savings and loan crisis."

FDIC public relations officer Alan Whitney: "[All estimates] were based on the best information available at those times. It is clear that economic conditions changed over the time."

The tension is also illustrated by the open ridicule that top Federal Reserve and Treasury officials have heaped on specific elements of FDICIA and their open contempt for the act's efforts to reduce regulatory discretion. They seize virtually every opportunity they can to rein-force industry concerns about excessive regulatory burdens and to communicate their own reluctance to implement several of its provis-ions (for example, use of stock-market values in assessing soundness and the need to set loan-to-value standards for mortgage loans). Such comments constitute a second line of FOF mischaracterizations, exag-gerations, and distortions that deserve review.

Several FDICIA initiatives have been unfairly characterized as bank-bashing exercises. One initiative that seems to me to ask authorities to treat divergences between the market value of a bank's stock and the book value of its net worth as a covenant-like signal of hidden prob-lems has been openly mocked by the Federal Reserve. The Fed's re-quest for public comment on this initiative frames the issue as if Con-gress had asked bank regulators to control bank stock prices. The questions the Fed posed are laden with sarcasm and plainly invite respondents to hold the provision up to ridicule.

Federal banking regulators are so far stubbornly refusing to ac-knowledge what Congress has clearly grasped: that the lessons of the S&L insurance mess apply to the banking regulators and the BIF. In asking for detailed regulatory norms, Congress is not "bashing" banks. It is telling regulators to develop enforceable standards of regulatory performance. Such standards would force regulators to leave a clear "audit trail" for regulatory decisions that effectively waive taxpayer covenant rights. Taxpayers and Congress need such standards and audit trails to make top regulators accountable for deposit insurance losses that accrue during their watch (as opposed to losses that are discretionarily realized then).

THE FALSE TEST OF A "DECEMBER SURPRISE"

Reluctance to disclose problem situations and to take tough disciplin-ary actions against an agency's regulatory clientele lies at the heart of the deposit insurance problem. This is what makes the situation a "mess" rather than a "crisis." The need for regulatory action is hidden and the cumulative effects of repeatedly deferring needed actions are misrepresented. The result is that public policy experts end up debat-ing whether action is truly needed rather than focusing on hammering out effective programs of action. Fears of a "December surprise" simi-larly misframe the central issue in the mess. Treated as a test for indus-

TABLE 1. *Major Differences between Benston-Kaufman/Shadow Financial Regulatory Committee Proposal and FDICIA*

Item	Benston-Kaufman/Shadow Financial Regulatory Committee Proposal	FDICIA
Number of capital zones	>10 percent market value leverage	>8 percent book value risk-based >5 percent book value leverage (tier 1)
Capital ratio for required resolution	3 percent market value	2 percent book value tier 1
TBTF exemption to least cost resolution	No	Limited
Expected losses to FDIC	0	< 2 percent except for TBTF
Final resolution	Immediate	Some delay
Fed discount window loans to undercapitalized bank	With approval of FDIC or uncollateralized	Limited
Deposit insurance premiums	Risk-based, but ineffective without "closure" rule	Risk-based in package with "closure" rule
Carrot in carrot-stick incentive structure	More powers, more freedom, less hassle	Same, plus lower insurance premiums
Subordinated debt	Important component of capital	Role delegated to regulators

try weakness, this idea focuses on the sideshow of forecasting regulators' highly politicized decisions about whether and when to "fail" or recapitalize economically insolvent banks instead of on measuring and controlling the unbooked losses to which the BIF exposes the federal taxpayer.

This summer, I estimated that, as of December 31, 1991, BIF's net loss exposure might amount to $53 billion. Applying the same estimation methods to June 30, 1992, data for banks as computed by the bank-analysis firm Veribanc, BIF's position improved to between $45 and $50 billion.

However, on the basis of net-worth and earnings data, Veribanc sorts banks into categories patterned after the colors of the standard traffic light. The 1,067 doubtful banks that fall into what Veribanc calls its red, yellow, and very light green categories correspond roughly to the 1,044 problem banks identified by the FDIC. As table 1 shows, the bulk of BIF's unbooked loss exposure lies in two seriously distressed yellow categories. Like a yellow traffic light, their condition should signal a halt to toleration of their weakness. Many of these banks are deeply economically insolvent, even though their accounting ratios are not yet desperate enough to force federal regulators either to demand recapitalization or to impose other mandatory disciplines. The danger of their future average deterioration from perverse risk-taking incentives leads me to offer an alternative, larger estimate of BIF's unbooked loss exposure of $54.5 billion.

The electorate must understand that there could only have been a surprise this December if it came from the policies of the new president and new Congress. It could not come from the tangible capital trigger set by FDICIA. Scheduling a life-and-death exam one year ahead and making the right answer to the test question known in advance gave zombie firms ample opportunity to cram effectively for the test. Those that could not recapitalize themselves straightforwardly have been drawing on whatever accounting options they could find to nudge their capital ratio above the 2-percent threshold. Troubled banks' interest in locating on the edge of the regulatory trip wire minefield explains why the seriously distressed yellow categories in table 1 are so full. Exercising sharp accounting options is, of course, easier when test administrators are anxious not to see too many weak "students" embarrass themselves.

This fall, Veribanc found banks to be rapidly migrating from the list of "critically undercapitalized" institutions it maintains. By late October, a more aggressive closure policy and regulatory relief had reduced the list to forty-one banks with $10.6 billion in assets. Interestingly, several escapees made it over the wall because of special agreements with the agencies that served to qualify selected categories debt instruments as regulatory capital. By early December, the list had fallen to about twenty banks with only about $6 billion in assets. In October, Veribanc estimated that only another 146 banks with $38 billion in assets were probably in the "undercapitalized" or "significantly undercapitalized" regulatory zones that trigger lesser disciplines.

Not observing a spurt in bank failures or recapitalizations either in the wake of the November 3 election or when FDICIA's 2-percent capital threshold kicks in tells us more about regulatory faintheartedness than about the extent of economic insolvency in the banking industry. In the meantime and probably for months to come, a disturbing number of undercapitalized deposit institutions are free to book short-funded positions in Treasury securities without recapitalizing themselves. Indeed, the weighting pattern used in the risk-based capital system encourages this. These positions are speculative gambles on the course of future interest rates for which taxpayers are unconscionably being made to hold the downside. Even if the managers and stockholders of these institutions end up winning their bets, taxpayers are financing their speculations on an interest-free basis.

Top regulators' penchant for discussing hardheaded insolvency resolution as a policy that would "close down the industry" disgracefully distorts the recapitalization issue. Just as in a private restructuring, no government supervisor should liquidate an insolvent institution whose franchise can be shown to be valuable enough for it to continue operation. If a troubled, but viable, firm's stockholders refuse to recapitalize the enterprise, their position should be closed out. While supervisors search for new private investors to take over the bank, the FDIC should routinely seek to offset BIF's loss exposure with a carefully balanced claim on the firm's future cash flows.

THE FRAUDULENT BENEFITS CLAIMED FOR PROJECTED BIF ACCOUNTING PROFITS

Anyone who has helped a loved one face cancer knows that denying that a problem exists is less painful in the short run than confronting that problem head on. But it is dramatically less beneficial as well. Any thinking person should be disturbed by the economic benefits the FDIC and banking trade-association spokespersons claim for FDIC projections of the net "accounting income" that BIF can generate from future premium receipts. These projections are being used to allege that the BIF can recapitalize itself over time by charging relatively safe banks an excessive price for FDIC services. In turn, the allegation that BIF's capital shortage will vanish over time by itself is being used to justify a policy of benignly neglecting the economic insolvency of hundreds of weak banks.

Analyses of BIF loss exposure that forecast large amounts of future net premiums are conceptually flawed. Premiums and additions to reserves should be calculated net of the insurer's loss exposure in each client. Economic theory indicates that setting premiums high above their value to low-risk bank clients is bound to increase BIF's contingent loss exposure. As the Shadow Financial Regulatory Committee has emphasized, burdensome premiums create a virtually irresistible incentive for low-risk institutions to expand their risk-taking to make sure that the value of the insurance services they receive from BIF equals or exceeds the charge the FDIC levies on them.[3] This insight clarifies that, in equilibrium, the present value of BIF's future net premiums must be zero. Moreover, it is easy for an institution to expand its risk-taking; for example, by securitizing or collateralizing strong assets or by mismatching the futurity of an institution's assets and liabilities. This means that any transitional benefits to BIF reserves from raising premiums are bound to dissipate quickly.

Putting off the insolvency resolution of crippled banks and using accounting games to suggest the possibility of a painless recapitalization for BIF are faithless actions that strongly capitalized institutions and other informed parties ought to protest. For BIF to become truly self-financing, it is not enough to rebuild its reserves in an accounting sense. Although it can price and police its services to avoid future losses, outside resources must be tapped to overcome the imbedded losses that represent the effects of past forbearance policies. Resources to cover past losses can only be collected through taxes of some kind. If temporarily very profitable survivor banks are truly going to be asked to share the recapitalization burden with the general taxpayer, Congress had best plan to enact a one-time special tax assessment against bank income or assets.

NOTES

1. Federal Deposit Insurance Corporation, Department of the Treasury, and Federal Reserve System, *Risk-Based Capital Standards: Joint Advance Notice of Proposed Rule Making*, 12 C.F.R. 325, 12 C.F.R. 3, and 12 C.F.R. 208, 225 (1992).

2. Shadow Financial Regulatory Committee, *Rule Proposed by Bank Regulators to Control Interest Rate Risk*, Statement 87 (September 14, 1992).

3. Shadow Financial Regulatory Committee, *The FDIC's Proposed Schedule of Risk Sensitive Premiums*, Statement 83 (June 1, 1992).

JAMES ANNABLE

Comments

I had three general problems with this assignment. First, comments are short whereas the issue is complex. Second, I am an economist turned banker, producing a certain mopishness on the subject of regulation. Third, I did not receive the papers by Karen Shaw and Kenneth Scott. This last fact provides me the latitude to make a more general comment about FDICIA and deposit-insurance regulation.

THE KEY PROBLEM

The "market" for deposit insurance is inefficient. The distribution of relevant information between the regulators and the regulated is inherently unbalanced, to the disadvantage of the regulators. This is generally true in ongoing regulatory systems. A fundamental policy issue in regulation (often ignored) is whether the costs of regulation, imposed to offset information asymmetries, exceed the benefits of regulation.

FDICIA: A DESCRIPTION

The best way to understand FDICIA is as the latest step in the dynamic process produced by information asymmetries associated with deposit insurance. From that perspective, it has four key elements:

—Prompt corrective action (the by-the-book regulatory interventions linked to capital-asset ratios),

—Risk-based deposit-insurance premiums (linked to capital-asset ratios),

—Least-cost resolution of bank failures (including sharp limitations on the doctrine of "too big to fail"), and

—A collection of cost increases on banks, prohibitions on bank activities, and mandated studies (the results of which will lead to increased costs and more proscribed behavior).

The purpose of the FDICIA is to protect the federal deposit insurance fund. It is important to remember that the purpose of the original deposit-insurance legislation was to improve the efficiency of the deposit-taking system.

REGULATORY DYNAMICS

Many years ago, in the academic phase of my career, when I was publishing primarily to avoid perishing, I spent some time looking at trucking regulation. My analysis described a simple dynamic feedback process. The regulators at the Interstate Commerce Commission (ICC) adjusted prices and entry to produce a target operating ratio (the ratio of operating costs to operating revenues); subsequent increases in the operating ratio were expropriated by the Teamsters in the form of higher wages and benefits, pushing the actual operating ratio below the target. The regulators then attempted to raise the ratio, and the process continued. The major outcomes of the regulatory process were accumulating inefficiencies and some well-paid truckers.

Feedback dynamics are an important feature of regulatory systems. Moreover, dynamic systems that are constructed on inherent information asymmetries between the regulators and the regulated tend to produce inefficiencies. Rational behavior on the part of the regulated requires that they recognize their regulatory environment and adjust to it.

In deposit-insurance regulation, four interrelated characteristics of the feedback dynamics are noteworthy.

—The operative goal of the regulators has become the protection of the deposit insurance fund, not the original goal of improving the efficiency of the deposit-taking system.

—The objective of the feedback game is to "find the risk." The regulators want to protect the insurance fund by reducing system risk. The principal value added of banks is absorbing and transforming financial risk; that function, as illustrated by the rapid development of derivative products and markets, can be accomplished in a wide variety of ways. The regulators will necessarily lag in the "find-the-risk" dynamic. (Consider, in illustration of the inherent lag, that C&I loans continue to be a single homogeneous category for calculating risk-based capital requirements.)

—The feedback system inefficiencies are mounting:

a. The costs of regulation are accumulating. (One recent survey of banks estimated the compliance costs for the pre-FDICIA system of regulation at nearly $11 billion a year.)

b. Behavior changes in order to adjust to the regulatory system. (Consider two examples of rational changed behavior. Government securities, which conserve capital in the current capital-driven regulatory environment, are now 22 percent of total bank assets—up from 15 percent five years ago. Commercial and industrial loans are now about 21 percent of total assets—down from 25 percent five years ago. In addition, the prime lending rate spread over the cost of funds has increased dramatically since 1990, up roughly 100 basis points.)

—The rising regulatory costs are being largely borne by smaller businesses and households.

POLICY IMPLICATIONS

Given the narrow goal of protecting the deposit insurance fund, the FDICIA is a productive step. It identifies and compensates for some of the perverse incentives that have developed in the regulatory system over time. In the larger context of the efficiency and effectiveness of the financial system, however, FDICIA (as the latest step in the ongoing dynamic feedback process) will fail. My judgment is that the costs of regulation (to protect the insurance fund) already exceed the benefits of deposit insurance.

I believe that, when the accumulating inefficiencies become too burdensome, public policy will turn to some version of the sheltered bank. In effect, depository institutions will be provided a choice. They can choose to retain federal deposit insurance, in which case their investments would be restricted to a limited menu of low-risk assets. Or they can choose to forego government deposit insurance and be free to select any mix of assets.

Short of sheltered banks, I have another proposal. To help overall efficiency, put the banking regulatory process on a "pay-as-you-go" budget, similar to the congressional fiscal procedures adopted in 1990. Specifically, every new page of regulations would be paid for by eliminating a page of existing regulations. Every process needs some sort of discipline.

Two Views from the
Policymaking Community

The Future of the Banking Industry

No nation's economy can be robust without healthy credit intermediaries.

The bad news of the 1980s—the multibillion dollar S&L debacle—has proven to be not only an embarrassment to Washington and a liability to the taxpayer, but because of compensating new regulation, has precipitated constraints on future private sector initiative. The good news of the 1990s is that the American banking system could, in short order, become the strongest in the world, if Congress faces up to the mistakes of the past without flinching from its responsibilities or, in an overreaction, imposing undue and, in some cases, improper burdens on financial institutions.

Key to the immediate future is understanding the immediate past. Savings and loan insolvencies were precipitated by macroeconomic mismanagement. The Carter inflation robbed all institutions that borrowed short and lent long, most particularly thrifts, of their net worth. The congressionally sanctioned Reagan deregulation exacerbated the problem by allowing unprecedented leveraging and unpardonable powers in an industry lacking capital and, in too many instances, ethics.

Many Americans are asking the question: Could the banking industry go the way of the savings and loan industry—that is, bust?

The answer is an unqualified "no" if three assumptions are made: (1) the new administration marshals the discipline to refuse to fall prey to the "programmatists" who have been out of the executive branch but not out of power the last twelve years; (2) the new regulators recognize that the most prudent way to protect the taxpayer, establish a level competitive playing field, and serve the economy is to emphasize institutional capital strength and responsible leveraging ratios instead of nit-picking microregulation; and (3) the economy doesn't slip into a deepening recession.

The bond market will be the first critic of Clinton economic policy.

If Wall Street and European bond traders believe that the new administration is attempting capriciously to spur economic growth through expanded deficit spending, they will dump bonds on the market, causing bond prices to fall and interest rates to rise. The collapse in bond prices will decimate the fixed interest rate portfolios of banks and thrifts. Given the recent extraordinarily favorable interest rate environment and the crowding effect of Washington's deficits, banks have become enormous investors in government securities. They now hold more securities in their portfolios than commercial loans. These portfolios have reduced credit risks for banks, but have also made bank profits vulnerable to interest rate swings.

Generally speaking, as reflected in capital ratios, good banking today is in inverse relation to size and, as reflected in the quality of loan portfolios, in inverse relation to proximity to the coasts and number of Harvard MBAs on staff. In the 1960s and 1970s the assumption was that big banks required relatively less capital than smaller institutions because their loans were more diversified and their management more sophisticated. One of the unspoken lessons of the 1980s would appear to be counterintuitive to Washington: the larger is the institution, the more capital is necessary to manage risk. Not only do larger institutions appear to understand their customers less well than smaller ones—witness LDC, Trump, and Olympia and York lending—they appear to serve a borrowing base—big business—which is, relative to small business, less likely to grow and more likely to use competitive sources for raising capital. Hence, coming from weakness rather than strength, large banks can make a compelling case that their viability depends on expanding powers, breaking, in particular, Glass-Steagall.

Fortunately, as traditional lending has brought more liabilities than profits for a number of money center institutions, new sources of revenue have been found in such diverse areas as trust management and currency trading. Fortunately as well, America's largest banks are publicly traded corporations and as such are hallmarked by ready ability to raise capital the old-fashioned way—through equity offerings. It is a myth propitiated by bank management that for any of our largest twenty of thirty banks there are insurmountable obstacles to raising prudent levels of capital in the equity markets. What is not a myth is that in many instances bank management prefers not to dilute stock and risk raising the ire of current stockholders or losing control to newer ones. It is, however, the responsibility of government to insist that banks of any size with inadequate capital be recapitalized. Adequate levels of private capital not only protect the taxpayer, they put banks in a far better position to boost the economy by expanding their options to make entrepreneurial loans.

The irony is that recent regulation has militated against risk taking in general and entrepreneurial lending in particular. The Basle Accord, for instance, by requiring no leveraging offsets for government bond holding and reduced levels of capital for mortgage making, biases banks against commercial lending. For the sake of the economy, very different priorities would seem to be in order. It is hard to believe America can become competitive in the next century if our tax laws give incentives for commercial business to overleverage with leveraged buyouts (LBOs) and our banking regulation gives incentives for commercial banks to buy bonds instead of make loans.

Today, the biggest problem in banking relates more to the role of banks in strengthening the economy than to the role of the economy on the strength of banks.

While as many as 100 to 125 banks, approximately 1 percent of our nation's total, may have to be merged by the government into stronger institutions over the next year or two, the likelihood is that, absent renewed recession or financial chaos on the West Coast, the cost to the FDIC will be manageable. Banks currently are enjoying record profits and the average equity-to-assets capital ratio for the industry has increased to more than 7¼ percent—the highest level since 1966. More remarkably, a lower interest rate environment has produced record profits in the solvent portion of the thrift industry and decreased the liabilities of insolvent S&Ls. Albert Casey, head of the Resolution Trust Corporation (RTC), has even suggested (perhaps Pollyannaishly) that as little as $25 billion additional federal resources may be needed to finish the S&L cleanup. What the actual cost of stabilizing the thrift industry will be is uncertain; what is not is that it will mushroom if interest rates accelerate.

Carter policy precedents should not be lost on the new administration. In the late 1970s, the United States had to sell gold reserves to meet international obligations—issue "Carter bonds" in other counties' currencies—in order to borrow money overseas and to seek assistance from the International Monetary Fund—all steps usually reserved for third world countries.

The surprise for the banking industry is not a December 1992 one where, at a maximum, sixty to eighty banks may not meet the government's new 2 percent capital floor, but a December 1993 one where the FDIC may have to take over the remaining cost of the S&L bailout if Congress continues to refuse to provide the resources to meet its deposit insurance obligations. If Congress fails to act, commercial banks could be saddled with obligations not of their making. Disintermediation could be precipitated of such a massive dimension that scores more financial institutions could falter or fail.

During the 1970s and 1980s, commercial banks were paranoid about the coming competition of money center institutions symbolized by Citicorp and the nonbank banks symbolized by Sears. The first threat failed to materialize to the degree universally expected because of poor loan controls; the second, because of consumer resistance to nontraditional banking. My prediction is that the next decade will be characterized by growing competitive concern for government-sponsored enterprises (GSEs), particularly Fannie Mae and Freddie Mac, which have been granted a regulatory advantage over traditional banking institutions and legislated weaker standards.

The challenge for the new administration is to shift priorities, as it is committed to do, without radically increasing the deficit. Policy initiatives have thin margins of error. Even jobs policies, if too ambitious, could produce greater joblessness. An economy precariously straddled with a substantial debt overhang simply cannot afford a surge in interest rates.

While perhaps impossible to graph, I would suggest the existence of Leach's law of disorderly deficits whereby at some point a seemingly incremental increase in the deficit, whether precipitated by a tax cut or new program expenditure, has a cyclonic straw-breaking effect, so punishing to market confidence, so strangling of private savings that the cost of all borrowing quantumly escalates. The first casualty of fiscal ill-discipline is the private sector borrower, the second, the taxpayer, and the third, any financial intermediary that lacks the capacity to hedge or adapt lending rates quickly.

The new administration must come to grips with the fact that tomorrow's deficit problem is complicated by the failure of Congress to date to provide resources necessary to resolve yesteryear's thrift problem. A breach in Wall Street's confidence could be magnified by a breach in the public's. A no-growth economy punctuated by higher deficits and further delays in resolving issues in the financial community could not only increase thrift bail-out costs but prove so jolting to public confidence as to produce runs on financial institutions.

Despite lack of attention in the campaign, the first order of business of the new administration must be to address problems of the financial community. Here, luck may well be with President Clinton.

What is widely misunderstood is that banks can be profitable when the economy is in shambles. The Bush years can be characterized as a four-year retrenchment period in which our nation's public financing system weakened, but our private sector banking system stabilized— indeed, strengthened. In fact, despite nominal GNP growth, the recent macroenvironment has been so good for banks that 1992 is by all odds the most profitable in American history.

President Clinton thus has the unique opportunity to build on a much stronger and more stable financial system than Bush inherited. While Bush's challenge was to increase viability, if not survivability, of our banks, Clinton's is to devise ways the banking system can be incentivized to serve more aggressively the economy at large. If successful at this endeavor, all of the more ballyhooed public sector initiatives articulated in the campaign will pale in significance.

The key to economic growth, as contrasted with bank profitability, is to provide incentives for financial institutions to make loans to job-creating enterprises, not simply to inefficient government bureaucracies and job-reducing leveraged buyouts. This can be done only with more restrained federal spending, an investment-oriented tax policy, and a strongly capitalized banking system unhindered by regulatory micromanagement.

DAVID W. MULLINS, JR.

Capital Standards and the Performance of the U.S. Banking Industry

Some bankers these days complain that the industry is being regulated to death. Readers of the financial pages will find this an odd complaint, however. The U.S. banking industry had all-time record first-quarter profits in 1992, all-time record second-quarter profits, and all time record third-quarter profits; and this, of course, aggregates to all-time record profits equaling $24 billion so far for the year.

Barring a real December surprise, 1992 set the all-time record for industry earnings, perhaps more than $30 billion for the full year, compared with $18 billion last year. The average in the 1980s was about $14 billion. So far in 1992, the average return on assets is 96 basis points. Roughly two-thirds of U.S. banking institutions earned more than 1 percent on assets through the third quarter. In typical years, less than half earn more than 1 percent. There are still asset quality problems in the U.S. banking industry: $69 billion in nonperforming loans. But one has to measure that against $55 billion in reserves and $257 billion in equity capital.

The industry has made impressive progress in working through its asset quality problems. Over the four-and-three-quarters years from 1988 to 1992, the industry has charged off $123 billion in bad loans, yet increased reserves by $5 billion and added $77 billion in equity capital. As Congressman Jim Leach mentions in his paper, the capital base has been expanded with retained earnings and large equity issues producing an average equity capital ratio of 7.5 percent in 1992, up from 5.8 percent in the beginning of the 1980s, and, as Congressman Leach also notes, the highest since 1966. This capital is not just accounting fluff.

The stock market's view of the industry has changed dramatically as well. For the top fifty institutions at the end of 1990, the average market-to-book-value ratio was about 85 percent. Banking stocks were selling at a 15 percent discount to book value. Today, the top fifty are selling at a 61 percent premium to book value.

So, all in all I think it is clear that 1992 was the single best year in the entire history of the U.S. banking industry. One reaction to this performance is if U.S. banks are being regulated to death, what a way to go! I think this is the wrong reaction, for a couple of reasons. First, this is actually a tale of two industries. It is the best of times for most in the industry, but still the worst of times for too many. We continue to have a near record volume of assets on the FDIC's problem bank list, almost $500 billion, and the FDIC's BIF fund remains depleted, down from 18 billion in 1987. Second, I believe that the concern over the economic damage of regulatory burden is valid and the potential damage quite real.

It is true that bank failures have decreased in number and leveled off in size. Nonetheless, all is not well when roughly 15 percent of the industry's assets—half a trillion dollars—is in troubled institutions. These firms represent the residue that has fallen to the bottom of the industry, unable to compete in an increasingly competitive financial services industry revolutionized by technology and innovation. I will not review the sort of fundamental reform we need, but in my view we will continue to have weakness in the banking industry until we get that reform.

With the industry so traumatized by the results of last year's attempt at reform, it appears unable to enjoy even a record year. Consequently, it may be reticent to come back and ask for fundamental reforms in the very near term, and thus I am not so optimistic on that front.

So despite the profitability of the industry as a whole, there is still a weak segment that represents an economic and, in some sense, political threat. Congress focuses on the threat to the taxpayer, even though the bulk of the industry is doing well.

A second reason not to celebrate too much is the massive increase in regulatory burden in recent years. We have seen this firsthand at the federal banking agencies. Each agency had to create more than sixty working groups to write the regulations to implement FDICIA. In my view too many of the requirements of that statute represent a dead-weight economic loss, wasted resources imposed on the banking industry without measurable benefits to safety and soundness.

The cost of FDICIA has yet to show up in the industry, although some people could argue, I suppose, that, absent the increased burden, the industry may well have earned record profits in this financial environment with a lower prime rate and more lending. But I think the real economic burdens are in the future, as next year many of these requirements will be fully implemented.

There are also healthy components of FDICIA that we must not overlook. Prompt corrective action is a step forward, as are the foreign bank supervisory components of the act. Nonetheless, in my judgment the rising tide of regulatory burden, in the context of an environment of intense competition in financial services, does constitute a threat to the viability of the industry.

It is useful to ask: How did this happen? What did the industry do to inspire this sort of legislative assault? The answer is simple: The U.S. banking industry got too close to the taxpayers' pocketbook. In the wake of the S&L workout, a similar federal safety net for banks, a depleted insurance fund, and record assets in problem banks all motivated Congress to lower the regulatory boom on the banking industry.

How can the industry reverse this trend and convince Congress to reduce regulatory burden? One way is for the industry to move away from the taxpayers' pocketbook by limiting the scope of the federal safety net. Many participants in this conference have fresh bruises or old scars resulting from previous attempts to try to limit the federal safety net. I won't open any old wounds with suggestions on how to do this, but I will move on to the narrower issue of the repeal of the more notable FDICIA burdens.

FDICIA was a simple deal. Congress imposed heavy regulatory burdens, and in exchange Congress, for the first time, authorized the U.S. Treasury to set up a formal, direct, substantial funding mechanism for the FDIC insurance fund. So for the first time, Treasury funds, that is, taxpayers' funds, would be used to fund losses in the FDIC's bank insurance fund. The line of credit from Treasury to FDIC was raised from $5 to $30 billion.

Given the performance of the industry and the improved outlook for the economy, one wonders whether the industry would be willing to reverse the deal; to achieve a rollback in regulatory burden in exchange for taking the Treasury out of the business of funding the FDIC, reestablishing the Treasury line as a modest liquidity backup, rather than a substantial funding mechanism, and allowing the industry to once again take direct, frontline responsibility for funding the FDIC.

I will leave this question to others and turn to the question of the

Basle capital standards and their role in the recent behavior we have seen in banking institutions. Looking back to March 1989 and thinking about the Basle Accord, why was it done? The basic issue was competitive equity. Foreign institutions had low capital requirements and were competing unfairly, and, indeed, these low capital requirements helped contribute to worldwide excess expansion of credit. The retrenchment from that excess credit expansion is contributing to a world economic slowdown.

The risk-based framework is consistent with the basic tenets of finance. Riskier investments should be backed by more capital. This is consistent with observed market-induced capital structures in private industry. We see risky firms that have low debt ratios and high equity ratios. More stable firms, like utilities, tend to have high debt ratios or low equity ratios. It is also consistent with other regulatory capital schemes. The SEC's net capital requirements are heavily risk based, although they tend to be based upon marketability risk, not credit risk.

So the objective of a risk-based capital framework was, in part, to remove the bias toward risky investment that comes from having a single capital standard for risky investments as well as low-risk investments.

I should note that there was controversy in 1989 about applying these standards to domestic institutions. Some felt they should be applied only to international institutions. The concern was not that the Basle standards were too stringent, but that they were too weak. Some feared that if we applied the Basle standards to domestic institutions, it would substantially reduce capital standards for the U.S. banking industry.

That was a rather vigorous debate that continues today. The tentative outcome was to retain the leverage ratio in addition to risk-based standards.

It is a bit curious and ironic that now the allegation is that somehow the Basle standards imposed a burden on the banking industry that turned the industry away from lending and toward investment in government securities, producing a credit crunch with an alleged detrimental effect on the economy. The alternative explanation is that the underlying economic and financial conditions induced the change in bank behavior. The recession and the dramatic trend toward deleveraging reduced loan demand, and asset quality problems motivated banks to raise underwriting standards and shore up capital ratios and liquidity. This sort of behavior is typically associated with recessions. The severity might be related to the severe nature of the asset quality problems and excess leverage in this cycle.

I do not present a rigorous analysis here that will settle this issue, however, and although work has been done on it, no definitive conclusions have yet been found. I do propose to raise some questions and some issues that I think are important in the ongoing debate about the Basle capital standards. At the outset I would acknowledge that the Basle standards have had the effect of shifting bank investment away from riskier loans and toward safer securities. That is what they were designed to do—to remove the bias toward risky investment inherent in having a single capital standard for all risk level investments.

The question is was the Basle effect marginal, or was it substantially responsible for the large shift from loans to securities that we have observed. To answer, I would note several things. First, of course, the Basle standards are not now, nor have they ever been, binding on the overwhelming fraction of the industry. In fact, 98.5 percent of U.S. banks meet the risk-based standards, representing 98.8 percent of the assets. Even in December 1990, 95 percent of the industry met the standards.

The tier 1 capital requirement is 4 percent; the average U.S. bank has 9.6 percent. This is not close. The risk-based capital requirement is 8 percent; the average U.S. bank has almost 12 percent. And, indeed, even the well-capitalized standards are exceeded by most U.S. banks— 94 percent of U.S. banks meet the well-capitalized standards, and they represent almost 80 percent of industry assets. This is up from 88 percent of the institutions in December 1990 that met those standards.

Indeed, two-thirds of U.S. banks have risk-based capital greater than 14 percent against the 8 percent standard. So the Basle capital standards have not been binding on U.S. banks, nor did we expect them to be.

There is no question that U.S. banks did enter this period with inadequate capital, and they have raised capital. They felt pressure to raise capital well above the Basle standards. The pressure came not only from regulators, but banks felt real pressure from the markets. In the fall and winter of 1990, some institutions had to pay 500 basis points above the comparable Treasury rate to raise subordinated debt, and some institutions had to pay very high spreads on their money market preferred stock, and their stock prices fell as well. This was the market giving them a message to add capital. When the market does this, banks respond very quickly. Moreover, bankers also decided they needed more equity capital in order to be able to lend on a sustainable basis.

Should one blame the Basle standards when they do not appear to be a binding constraint? There is no question that there were higher constraints imposed by the market, the regulators, and the bankers themselves. It might be useful to look at the behavior of the least bound segment of the industry, the firms least likely to be motivated by the need to meet the Basle standards. If Basle is motivating bankers to acquire securities, that behavior should be less evident among those institutions that are least bound. But, to the contrary, the well-capitalized institutions—the ones with risk-based capital greater than 10 percent—account for the overwhelming majority of securities acquisitions over the last three years, despite the fact that they would not seem to have had to bias their investment behavior to meet the Basle standards.

What about a controlled experiment? Find a financial industry that is similar to banking but does not have risk-based standards imposed coincident with this economic cycle. I would suggest credit unions, as an example. They have traversed the same economic environment without risk-based capital standards. Their behavior has been somewhat similar to that of banks, except that they have cut back on their loans more dramatically and increased their securities more sharply than have commercial banks. Over the past four years, commercial banks' loans as a percentage of assets have fallen from 62 percent to 59 percent. Credit unions' loans to asset ratio has gone from 66 percent down to 55 percent during the same period. And credit unions have increased their investment in securities much more than banks. Treasury securities have risen from 10 to 15 percent of assets, and agencies or GSEs from 18 to 21 percent of credit union assets.

Though the shift is more dramatic, the pattern for credit unions lines up precisely with the timing observed for commercial banks. I suppose this could be a sympathetic reaction on the part of credit unions because of the imposition of Basle standards on banks. I do know that banks have no sympathy for credit unions, and I am not sure about the sentiment in the other direction.

The credit-union experience appears consistent with the view that weak demand and, perhaps, a concern about asset quality have been important factors behind the substitution of securities for loan growth; and I rather suspect that one would find similar patterns of behavior in other financial industries.

Thus, when one looks at unbound banks or unbound industries, this behavior is evident, so it seems difficult to ascribe too much of it to the Basle standards. And, of course, the timing isn't quite right either, because the standards were announced in March 1989 and one would expect banks to look ahead and dramatically cut lending and increase securities investment. Instead, banks continued to increase their lending as a percentage of their assets into late 1990 or early 1991. The cutback in loans seems to coincide with the economic cycle suggesting that economic fundamentals, more than Basle standards, were important causal factors.

Still, aren't banks in danger of becoming bond mutual funds? Let's put this in historical perspective. Fifty years ago the average bank had 60 percent of its assets in securities and 20 percent in loans. Today, those percentages are reversed. The average bank has brought securities down from 60 percent of assets to 15 to 20 percent of assets. Loans have increased steadily during this period, as banks' portfolios have, in effect, become riskier, even though their capital has not risen until recently.

Loans peaked as a percentage of assets at 62 percent in 1989 and 1990, and have fallen back to just under 59 percent. If banks are not lending enough, it can be said that they are lending more, as a percentage of their assets, than at any time in the past fifty years, and, I would suspect, any time in recorded history, except for a brief period from the mid-1980s through 1990, a period we now recognize as the tail end of a long period of overexpansion of credit.

Some of the pullback in lending is likely a cyclical response to that overexpansion of lending. Underlying this cyclical reversal is the cessation and perhaps some reversal of the long secular trend toward increased loan-to-asset ratios in U.S. banks.

Is this reversal likely to continue? Are banks likely to turn into mutual funds? It is difficult for banks to compete with bond mutual funds since banks average 400 basis points in noninterest expense. A good portion of that is intermediation costs. Mutual funds, of course, have very small intermediation costs.

Moreover, our evidence is that banks are not taking undue interest rate risk, that most of their investment is in the two-to-three-year maturity range. (I might add that the call report is misleading here because it puts all collateralized mortgage obligations (CMOs) into the five years and greater maturity category even though our evidence from surveys and supervisory experience suggests banks are investing in the shorter duration tranches of the CMOs.)

A 3 percent federal funds rate and a 5 percent three-year Treasury rate yield only a 200 basis point spread. I doubt that banks can recover their intermediation costs over the longer term with a strategy of investing in Treasury securities.

Compare this to small business lending: 2 percent above prime; a 500 basis points spread to Fed funds with no interest rate risk but credit risk. And, of course, consumer lending, for example credit card lending, also offers very attractive spreads compared to investing in Treasuries. It is also true that capital disadvantage of loans can be offset—our analysis would suggest—with about 50 basis points in additional return.

While securities investment may be a viable short-term holding strategy, even with a highly sloped yield curve, it is difficult for banks to consistently earn profits except through lending, and lending to segments of the market that do not have direct, cost-effective access to the public capital markets—lending where banks' expertise in credit evaluation and monitoring and in working with borrowers has value.

But isn't securities investment responsible for banks' impressive profit performance this year? So far in 1992, through the first three quarters, profit before tax in the banking industry totaled $35 billion, while securities gains were only $3.2 billion, less than 10 percent of industry earnings.

Of course, banks have also earned interest on their investment in securities. But when securities make up less than 22 percent of bank assets, they are destined to be only a sideshow in bank profitability. It should be clear that the source of banks' impressive profitability this year is the wider spreads on the 60 percent of their assets invested in loans.

The 300 basis point spread between prime and Fed funds is approaching a historical high. This is typical near the end of a recession, although it usually lasts only several quarters and it has lasted much longer this time. This persistently wide spread between loan rates and overall bank funding cost is consistent with weak loan demand, producing little payoff to loan rate competition and inducing banks to reduce deposit rates sharply.

Here is the case example of one large institution deeply into middle market lending. Earlier this year, this bank decided to get aggressive and cut its prime rate by a quarter point. The bank waited patiently to be trampled by credit-starved borrowers, but it got lonely after six weeks or so. The prime cut did not generate more borrowing; the bank simply lost a quarter point on all its existing prime-based loans. There is also ample survey evidence documenting weak loan demand from the National Federation of Independent Businesses and other sources.

Having said all this, I am not prepared to rule out the possibility that the Basle standards are misspecified and may have played more than an insignificant role in constraining lending. This is a legitimate subject for analysis. We should not shrink from rigorous, critical analysis of the Basle standards. To do this I would suggest that one needs a firm analytical foundation to secure an analytical anchor to the entire system. Then one can talk about relative standards.

I would propose, as the appropriate threshold question: Is 4 percent equity too high a capital requirement for investments of the risk level of commercial and industrial (C&I) loans? Is $4 behind every $100 of C&I loans too much to ask as the tier 1 equity requirement? And one can broaden the question. Is 8 percent total capital too high, or are 6 and 10 percent excessive as well-capitalized standards? These are important questions. We know the cost of getting these questions wrong.

Let's focus on the equity capital ratio. Is 4 or 6 percent too high? The history of loan losses as well as asset quality problems suggest that C&I loans are risky assets. This raises doubts as to whether 4 percent is too much to ask. And since the average bank has an overall ratio of equity to total assets of 7.4 percent, the industry does not seem to think the standard is too high. Also, we know the distortion caused by the federal safety net and the incentive to substitute the government guaranty for private capital and the risk associated with that.

So let's look at a similar industry without the federal safety net to see what capital structure the market induces. Commercial finance companies specializing in business loans exhibit equity capital ratios, comparable to tier 1 bank capital, in the 10 to 15 percent range. These firms are generally profitable, except for the few that followed banks into commercial real estate. They have been generally expanding their business loans during the recent period.

Moreover, there is an admittedly tenuous relationship between tier 1 equity and bond ratings that would tend to suggest that roughly a

10 percent ratio is associated with a strong investment grade bond rating. This is another market indication of appropriate bank capital structure.

Can banks be profitable at 10 percent equity? Finance companies are. Moreover, banks with the highest capital are the most profitable. There is interesting research on this relationship that I will not explore in this paper.

So there is a substantial burden of proof associated with the proposition that the problem with Basle is that the capital standards on C&I loans are too high and that this is an inappropriate constraint on bank lending.

What about the relative calibration of these standards? How about a zero capital requirement on government securities? This ratio is inappropriate; and we are in the process of designing interest rate risk standards to augment the basic Basle framework. In the interim the leverage ratio has been retained as a capital charge applying to all bank assets.

What about mortgage-backed securities at 20 percent weight? If $4 in equity behind every $100 in C&I loans is appropriate, how about 80 cents in equity capital behind every $100 in mortgage-backed securities as a cushion in case anything goes wrong with that $100?

There may be legitimate concerns about the relative calibration of these ratios, but we should be very careful not to allow dissatisfaction with the relative calibration of Basle ratios to lead us to the dubious and potentially very dangerous conclusion that we need to lower the absolute capital standards on risky lending. Having been down that road before we know that the first few miles are quite enjoyable, but the ultimate destination is very unpleasant.

If we attempt to treat the weakness in economic growth and in loan growth with the short-term narcotic of inappropriately low capital standards on risky lending, we know from the S&L experience that that is not a life-sustaining prescription for the industry or the economy.

I am not going to review the importance of the private capital ahead of the government guaranty as a protection for the taxpayer and as a constraint on moral hazard. As a former professor, I would hope that we learned that lesson last semester. If we haven't, we will certainly learn it again next semester; the question is whether we will ever graduate.

So, while there may be a question about the relationship of the Basle components, we ought to be careful to maintain an adequate capital requirement on risky lending.

Having raised these questions, the final question is: Is there a problem here at all? Or is all of this a natural, unavoidable adjustment process that the financial system and the economy must simply work its way through?

There is evidence of a problem here in the cumulative increase in burden on the industry. Equally important, there is troubling evidence with respect to C&I lending—small business lending, in particular.

Despite the long trend toward increased loans as a percentage of bank assets, C&I loans peaked, as a percentage of bank assets, in the late 1960s; and they have fallen during the 1980s from well over 20 percent of assets down to 15 percent. Total loans are still almost 60 percent of assets, much larger than securities. But C&I loans have fallen as a percentage of bank assets, and this started long before the Basle Accord. In contrast, consumer debt, mortgage debt, and mortgage-backed securities all rose sharply during the 1980s.

Perhaps this is a natural economic trend of securitization with the better C&I credits going directly to the markets. However, I think it warrants careful analysis. During the 1980s banks began to look less like business lenders and more like thrifts and consumer banks.

In the recent third-quarter data, bank loans increased after six consecutive negative quarters. Though overall loans increased, led by residential mortgages and consumer installment loans and home equity lines, C&I loans fell once again, this time by $6.5 billion.

There is also other evidence of tightness in business lending. Bank business loans (at U.S. offices) in late 1992 remained at about the same level as three years earlier in late 1989—a bit under $600 billion. During the same period, business lending by finance companies has expanded from about $250 billion to more than $300 billion. This suggests a substitution of finance company lending for bank lending. I doubt that this is a perfect substitution because finance companies focus on asset-based lending, as opposed to the generalized lending that banks do.

So looking at the trends, there is concern that the banking industry may be systematically retreating from small business lending in favor of mortgage and consumer loans. I have no doubt that in time, if this were true, alternative providers of finance would appear to fill the void. This may be happening. Some people would say that it might not be such a bad idea if this lending took place outside the federal safety net. However, this will take time, and there are adjustment costs to this process.

Why is small business lending so important? It is because small businesses are the chief source of growth for the economy, especially employment growth. During the decade of the 1980s, Fortune 500 companies reduced employment, and yet the economy produced almost 20 million new jobs. Small businesses are important contributors to economic growth and to job growth. But this segment is dependent, to a large extent, on bank financing, unlike other borrowers. Small businesses have relatively few financing alternatives, especially as a source of generalized finance.

The troubling longer-term trend in bank C&I lending suggests a couple of things. First, we need to know more about small business finance; we need more research into small business lending. Indeed, the Federal Reserve Board has approved and authorized a large sample staff research project into the nature of small business lending that will focus on the full range of financing available to small businesses, not just bank finance. This is a major research project that will take some time to complete.

As for the near term, it would be useful to carry out a systematic, rigorous analysis of the regulatory impediments to small business lending. Within the broader regulatory burden area we need to zero in on C&I lending. Then it would be useful to launch a search-and-destroy mission to eliminate unwarranted impediments.

There may be noncapital impediments. There has been a trend, culminating in FDICIA, toward standardization, the mechanism of supervision and regulation, with heavy emphasis on formulas, documentation, and rigid rules. This may have produced a systematic bias away from small business loans, which are often character loans, and cash flow loans, requiring judgment, active monitoring, and working with the borrower. These loans are heterogeneous in nature and may not be amenable to the increasingly standardized nature of supervision and regulation.

In contrast, this trend in regulation may bias lenders toward homogeneous lending product categories more easily documented, scored, and categorized, like mortgages and consumer loans. To understand the bias, consider the work a lending officer must do to document and qualify a cash flow loan to a small business without audited financial statements. Compare that to the easier task of placing funds in standardized mortgages or in consumer installment loans, amenable to computerized credit scoring. When one considers the difference in regulatory burden and documentation and especially the difference in examiner scrutiny between generalized small business lending and standardized mortgage and consumer lending, one wonders whether this could produce a systematic bias against business lending. There are also fixed costs involved. A small business loan requires much the same documentation as a loan to a Fortune 500 company.

So it is important to recognize the inherently different nature of business lending versus more standardized lending. For this segment it may be necessary to design a different regulatory process, tailored to be congruent with the nature of business lending, rather than trying to force business lending into the standardized, regulatory mold. Indeed, the SEC has reduced and simplified registration and reporting requirements for small securities issuers in the public capital markets. We should investigate whether there are appropriate analogs in the bank business lending area for reduced and simplified procedures.

Streamlined regulatory procedures for small business lending may cause some to worry about safety and soundness. I worry less as long as adequate capital standards are maintained for this type of lending. I would much prefer to depend upon capital standards than rely on noncapital regulatory processes. Of course, the capital standards themselves, I would admit, are legitimate targets in this analysis, especially the relative calibration of risk-based standards. But I believe a critical requirement of any examination or proposal to alter the capital standards should be a firm commitment to maintain adequate capital standards on risky lending. The objective should be to reduce the regulatory impediments to lending, while absolutely assuring that the banking industry is required to maintain adequate capital. It is important not just for the taxpayer but, as Congressman Leach states, for the economy. Capital standards that are too low produce overexpansion of credit and asset quality problems. Then, when weakness in the economy develops, banks must pull back to rebuild capital, exacerbating the downturn. This procyclical behavior is inherently destabilizing and damaging to the economy.

In contrast, a well-capitalized banking industry is able to lend on a sustainable basis, in good times and bad, to support the economy as a countercyclical force in a downturn.

Banks entered this recent period of economic weakness with weak capital and have incurred the economic cost of building bank capital in bad times. With a replenished capital base and ample liquidity, the U.S. banking industry appears now poised to support sustained economic growth. It would be indeed unfortunate if we dissipated these hard-won gains, attracted by the transitory thrill of yet another ride on the credit expansion rollercoaster.

The U.S. banking industry has made impressive progress in recent years. Weakness remains in a segment of the industry and weakness is likely to persist until fundamental banking reform is enacted. Despite the recent good performance, the rising tide of regulatory burden is a threat to the industry and ultimately to the economy. I would single out small business lending as a possible problem area, not just because of the Basle standards—after all, the same standard applies to consumer loans and business loans—but rather because of the longer term, troubling, downtrend in small business lending. Because of its importance to the economy this is an area worthy of rigorous analysis, leading perhaps to a redesign of the regulatory approach to small business lending, consistent with sound capital standards.

Responses to FDICIA: Banks and Regulators

JAY M. WEINTRAUB

FDICIA from the Bankers' Perspective: Too Much Medicine, Applied Indiscriminately

In my opinion as a twenty-year observer, the banking system is broken. It remains broken with the passage of FDICIA, which does nothing in terms of bettering industry efficiency and competitiveness. It does make it worse in some cases, though, and I would like to expand upon that.

Bankers accept regulation as a necessary cost of doing business as insured depositories, but the system of regulation has become overly expensive and unworkable. FDICIA is viewed by bankers as unnecessarily overreactive to the industry's troubles, as having injected the regulatory body deeply into the management of the banks, removing regulatory managerial discretions and replacing it with formulas for regulatory action.

Indeed, virtually everyone who understands the events of the 1980s in the banking industry understands the unfortunate facts leading to the passage of FDICIA. (1) The excesses of the 1980s exposed the fund to tremendous losses. The bank regulatory apparatus was unable to identify risk early and take effective action to prevent bank failures and losses to the fund. (2) Closing banks once book capital is exhausted assures a substantial loss to the deposit insurance fund. And, finally, (3) the primary purpose of FDICIA is to ensure that the banking industry will never again make a call on the U.S. Treasury.

Steps clearly needed to be taken to ensure that problem banks become subject to increasingly tight regulation and restrictions as the risk of failure increases. The key here is the term "problem banks," because it is problem banks that should be so treated, not the entire industry. FDICIA accomplished this goal, which banks generally support, but it failed in terms of balance and in addressing the long-term structural problems of the industry. As such, FDICIA was a realization of the punitive side only of needed banking reform. In a speech last month, Edward Kelly, a member of the Federal Reserve Board of Governors, referred to this problem as presenting the stick but not the carrot, a viewpoint widely held among those in the banking industry.

The banking industry clearly needs the removal of noncompetitive undercapitalized banks that bid up the cost of funds. Risk-based capital and deposit premiums are hardly controversial. But let us not be fooled by the current state of bank earnings. The industry simply cannot afford greater regulatory costs in addition to an environment that has increasingly favored nonbank competitors.

It is clear that the burden of compliance with FDICIA will be substantial, particularly in terms of audit fees and personnel time—personnel for compliance, as well as legal and line staff. And for what? The purpose, really, is to ensure compliance with safety-and-soundness objectives that are not startling in their scope or character. These are longstanding objectives from a regulatory point of view. What is new is that the broad spectrum of banks, largely well managed and healthy, will be made to absorb an increased level of regulatory cost, as a result of the failure of hundreds of mostly smaller banks, and, of course, the travails of the thrift industry.

The question is: Will the cure kill the patient? Banking has always been a highly competitive industry with relatively thin margins and earnings, when compared with nonbank competition. Banks have had to bear the costs of regulation and restrictions, as well as socially motivated requirements, such as CRA and disclosure rules not imposed on nonbanks.

The effect of that cost cannot be detected directly, but there is disturbing evidence in the marketplace. Bank customers have increasingly sought alternative sources of financing and deposit services in recent years, indicating banks' eroding competitiveness. How can FDICIA do anything other than accelerate that process? Regulation in general has finally been perceived as reaching overkill throughout the economy, as exemplified by President-elect Clinton's initiative on regulatory reduction. But what about in banking, arguably the most highly regulated business of all?

New regulations should have the burden to prove that their benefits outweigh their costs, not the other way around. The fact is there is no certainty that banks will continue to serve their traditional role of financial intermediation. It would be a mistake to take that notion for granted in piling on new regulatory requirements.

So what are the specific problems with FDICIA? Let me first mention the short-term issues. First, bank regulation, at its core, really is subjective and cannot be made objective. FDICIA ignores that reality and tries to mandate action that removes regulatory discretion, particularly in areas such as bank closures.

Ironically, to me, FDICIA also proceeds to dispense broad discretion in its ability to reclassify banks' capital zones, which is pretty scary. In reality, however, the capital level is largely a function of the subjective judgments made by examiners in reviewing the loan portfolios. And I know—I was there once as a field bank examiner. In fact, this goes back to what Ed Kane stated, which is that capital really is accounting. And what is bank accounting but examination?

Second, operational and managerial standards put regulators too deeply into the management of the industry itself. Do we want examination and regulation by bean counters' endless checklists? That is what is being proposed. The regulators themselves see portions of FDICIA as unneeded and unnecessarily intrusive on bank managements, such as the limits on executive compensation. For the most part, the regulators have had sufficient power, particularly in the post-FIRREA period, and have acted to reduce the burden caused by FDICIA in their enabling regulations.

Perhaps even more important are the unnecessary costs and duplication in compliance terms for the industry. Areas singled out for the greatest criticism by banks involve the costs in the truth-and-savings compliance, audit requirements, and new disclosures, such as those regarding lending to small businesses.

These and other provisions are costly, especially on smaller banks, and the regulatory burden is now a crushing weight. John Laware estimated an additional $4 billion in regulatory, audit, and other costs under FDICIA. Who will pay for this? Ultimately, customers will, either directly through higher charges or through reduced or eliminated services.

Likewise FDICIA did not directly address the long-term structural problems of the industry: unfair competition from the unregulated nonbanks, too many banks, outmoded regulatory barriers, and an inefficient and expensive delivery system.

FDICIA also establishes the well-capitalized level as a minimum, effectively ratcheting up the standards for capital, and leading to a need for an additional capital cushion. This, of course, was referred to earlier in the context of the potential effect of excessive capital. While we can draw some comfort in the higher capital creating fortress banks that we see today, ever higher capital is making the industry increasingly noncompetitive.

To illustrate, the sixty-three banking companies in the Merrill Lynch bank peer group were able in the aggregate to earn more than an 11 percent return on equity (ROE) on average in only one of the last five years. Earnings this year are better but still only in the 12.5 percent range, hardly awe-inspiring. Even with the record-setting earnings performance to date this year, return on equity remains below the long-term ROE goals of most banks.

While capital ratios have grown, in large measure by the substitution of U.S. Treasury securities for loans, this is not a desirable long-term trend. Of course, capital that goes up can come down when the banks eventually substitute loans for zero-risk U.S. Treasury securities.

There are other consequences, some perhaps unintended. First of all, FDICIA reduces the potential for recovery for banks experiencing financial problems. Not only will some banks fail that could have recovered, but also the liquidity constraints that are embodied in FDICIA could lead to unnecessary downward spirals for some banks that could have survived. These liquidity constraints include provisions limiting the market in brokered deposits, interbank funding, and the use of the discount window. Even the required use of the least-cost method of bank resolution could result in much higher volatility in uninsured deposits, which are likely to flee to strong banks—especially those still considered too big to fail—with unknown consequences on individual banks and the system as a whole. It was not a pleasant experience in 1989 and 1990 when bank holding companies had to pay 500 basis points over Treasuries to access the long-term debt market.

New rules will also make it difficult to attract and retain qualified directors. The FDIC already has had to assert that it will be reasonable in pressing claims against directors of failed banks. Thinking back to some of the revisions in the Southwest Plan and the treatment of regulatory goodwill for thrifts, if you were in the seat of the prospective director, would you read those lips?

What can be done in the short term to meet the legitimate needs embodied by FDICIA and improve the banking industry's competitiveness? Obviously, reduce the regulatory burden in FDICIA and seek or encourage modifying elements of the rules. Of course, we are seeing that already in terms of real estate lending standards and the interbank funding rules. We need to reorganize the industry, including consolidation, obviously, and also restructure the regulatory apparatus. We need to end duplications and inefficiencies in both. We need to apply FDICIA on a consolidated basis to reduce the cost of compliance for multibank holding companies or legalize nationwide banking, which, of course, would be even better.

In the long term we must not let the current high earnings in the industry allow us to ignore the structural problems that remain. If we go back to the Financial Institutions Subcommittee of the House Banking Committee report, it says, "Congress could and should minimize future bank failure costs, both by enhancing regulatory and market discipline against excessive risk taking and creating new opportunities for cost reductions and profits in the banking industry."[1]

We certainly have enhanced discipline with FDICIA in place. We must now improve the profit opportunities. Congress has given banks the medicine but not the cure. We need interstate banking legislation, which is really the only solution to the industry's long-term structural problems of excess capacity and insufficient diversification.

Everyone in the industry is being penalized for the sins of a relative few. The vast majority of banks remain healthy, and, just as risk-based deposit insurance makes sense in terms of placing the onus on the outlyers, it is foolish to punish all of the players with the harsh burdens of FDICIA.

I also would like to say that, in some of the papers, there has been an insufficient discussion of the difference between banks and thrifts. Banks are clearly paying today for the mistakes of the thrifts in the 1980s.

I am often asked how the financial markets are reacting to FDICIA. It is really too early to tell. I don't believe that the market will react until its effects are tangible, for example, when a bank fails or when the effects of some of these liquidity constraints become more obvious. And, of course, the banks are now doing quite well. But any action that reduces the competitiveness of banks, in my opinion, will eventually lead to lower prices for bank securities, both debt and equity.

I favor the use of more subordinated debt in the capital structure, which was mentioned earlier. That may sound somewhat self-serving, of course, coming from an employee of Merrill Lynch. But, on the other hand, if indeed we do use 4 percent and 8 percent capital level minimums for tier 1 and total capital under the Basle agreement, then there is no reason why a portion of the excess above that cannot have its purpose served by using subordinated debt, which would provide the ultimate market discipline.

I also would second the call for better disclosure. The light of day will help restrain some of the actions of management and help analysts better serve their function of bringing meaningful thought and perspective to the market.

In summary, we need to decide what we want our banks to be. Do we want them to be underperforming extensions of the government, providing mandated social services? Or, do we want them to be fully competitive with a wide range of nonbanks and foreign banks, from the point of view of industry efficiency and competitiveness.

I believe that FDICIA is a giant step in the wrong direction toward that important goal.

NOTES

1. James Barth, Dan Brumbaugh, and Robert Litan, "The Banking Industry in Turmoil, A Report on the Condition of the U.S. Banking Industry and the Bank Insurance Fund," report to the Financial Institutions Subcommittee of the House Banking Committee, December 17, 1990.

RICHARD SCOTT CARNELL

The Culture of Ad Hoc Discretion

My topic is "the culture of ad hoc discretion"—a viewpoint that permeates and helps embitter the debate over the FDICIA. The culture of ad hoc discretion condemns FDICIA's limitations on regulatory discretion. The argument goes something like this. Congress blundered when it limited regulators' discretion by enacting provisions like prompt corrective action and least-cost resolution. Such rules met no real need. Thrift regulators had ample discretionary powers to prevent a $200 billion thrift debacle. Bank regulators likewise had ample powers to head off bank problems while the FDIC's bank insurance fund was still the largest deposit insurance fund in the history of the world. Yes, regulators made inadequate use of those powers, but that just means we need better regulators, not rules limiting regulatory discretion. The problem did not lie in the pre-FDICIA system—only in the people running the system. So Congress made a huge mistake last year. Regulators should now interpret and implement FDICIA to maximize their own discretion and minimize FDICIA's effects.

Those who take this view regard FDICIA as simply a large collection of unwanted rules. In so doing, they miss the real point of the legislation.

I briefly describe how the pre-FDICIA system of federal deposit insurance and depository institution regulation (for brevity, "the old system") created perverse incentives for insured depository institutions' owners, managers, and regulators, and how FDICIA's key reforms mitigate those incentives. I'll then analyze the attitudes and assumptions underlying the culture of ad hoc discretion, point to its internal inconsistency, and note how it has distorted the debate over implementing FDICIA.

PERVERSE INCENTIVES OF THE PRE-FDICIA SYSTEM

The old system inadvertently encouraged depository institutions' owners, managers, and regulators to act in ways that harmed the insurance funds. It created perverse incentives for owners and managers to take excessive risks and for regulators to forbear and overextend the federal safety net. FDICIA's most important reforms—such as prompt corrective action, risk-based premiums, and least-cost resolution—represent a coherent effort to ameliorate those perverse incentives.[1]

Owners and Managers

Owners and managers faced (and continue to face) "moral hazard"—the tendency for insurance to encourage the persons insured to take greater risks than they would without insurance. Under the old system, all institutions paid premiums at exactly the same rate, meaning that safe institutions subsidized risky institutions. Moreover, deposit insurance and the related policy of treating some banks as "too big to fail" impaired market discipline, permitting weak institutions to remain open and compete aggressively with healthy institutions. Weak institutions tended to pay higher-than-average rates to attract deposits, and to channel the proceeds into riskier-than-average investments. This behavior was a rational response to the incentives created by the combination of flat-rate deposit insurance, limited liability, and low capital: if the risk-taking paid off, the institutions' owners kept the profits and their managers kept their jobs; if it failed, the insurance fund bore the loss.

But this behavior harmed healthy institutions. It squeezed net interest margins both by increasing the cost of funds and by decreasing interest rates on loans. It undermined credit standards by making credit more freely available to marginal borrowers. Too much money chased too few bankable loans, and lenders received inadequate compensation for credit risk. The erosion of credit standards increased loan losses and depository institution failures. The failures depleted the insurance funds, necessitating higher premiums that further undercut healthy institutions' profitability.

The point is not that we should have a risk-free system but that risky institutions should internalize their costs—they should not be able to dump them onto healthy institutions or the taxpayers. The incentives of the old system were perverse because they saddled the insurance fund with extra risk that it wasn't being paid to bear.

Ameliorating those perverse incentives will create a better operating environment for all depository institutions. It isn't punitive; it's highly constructive.

Regulators

The old system also created perverse incentives for regulators to practice forbearance, by which I mean failing to take *needed* action to correct a depository institution's problems.

As Edward Kane has pointed out, regulators' reputations suffer less for problems that actually develop on their watch than for problems that come to light on their watch. By confronting problems, regulators risk blame for causing them.[2] They also face a classic case of special-interest politics. Forbearance provides obvious short-term benefits to troubled institutions' owners and managers. The damage done to healthy institutions or the taxpayers is long-term and inconspicuous. So when regulators get tough, the people who stand to lose become incensed, while the people who stand to benefit hardly notice. Forbearance, although against the interests of the insurance fund, may well serve regulators' self-interest.

Acknowledging that regulators face perverse incentives is no criticism of regulators. On the contrary, it helps explain why regulators' jobs are so difficult. With a proper understanding of the incentives, one can work to mitigate them.

Some people question whether incentives to forbear still pose any problem. After all, during the past several years, bank and thrift supervision has become more stringent in response to public concern about the insurance funds' heavy losses. While this concern lasts, it helps counter perverse incentives, but it does not eliminate them, and it yields erratic results. Symbolism satisfies the concern as easily as substance. An agency can get better reviews from a single showy enforcement action than from twenty cases of forbearance avoided, even if avoiding forbearance does far more good than the symbolic enforcement. Enforcement is easy to understand and has minimal political costs, while avoiding forbearance is obscure and risks sharp industry criticism. This puts a premium on slamming the barn door after the horse is gone, rather than latching it in the first place. We need a system that will control excessive risk-taking without depending on a wave of public indignation and without imposing the regulatory equivalent of a prison lockdown.

FDICIA AS A PARTIAL ANTIDOTE TO PERVERSE INCENTIVES

FDICIA's deposit insurance reforms seek to bring the incentives of owners, managers, and regulators more closely into line with the interests of the insurance fund. I'll take as examples prompt corrective action, risk-based premiums, and least-cost resolution.

Prompt Corrective Action

Prompt corrective action imposes increasingly stringent restrictions and requirements as an institution's capital declines below required levels. For example, an undercapitalized institution cannot pay dividends, a significantly undercapitalized institution must normally recapitalize by selling stock or merging with a healthy institution, and a critically undercapitalized institution faces closure or sale. These rules strengthen owners' and managers' incentives to maintain adequate capital and cure any capital deficiency expeditiously. They also reduce the danger that capital deficiencies or risky behavior will go unchecked. By reducing losses to the deposit insurance fund, the rules will reduce the subsidy weak institutions can exact from healthy institutions, and thus reduce the moral hazard of deposit insurance.

To ameliorate regulators' incentives, the statute specifically requires regulators to take timely, effective action to prevent loss to the insurance fund—and holds regulators accountable for any failure to do so. The rules limit regulators' discretion to forbear, but are hardly draconian. Only a few of the rules allow no exceptions—notably those requiring a capital-restoration plan and restricting dividends and asset growth. And experience indicates that such stringency will promote the recovery of troubled but viable institutions.

Risk-Based Premiums

FDICIA requires the FDIC to establish a system of risk-based insurance premiums. Proportioning premiums to risk would align the incentives of owners and managers with the interests of the insurance fund. Risky institutions would internalize the costs of their risk-taking. Even a system that only roughly correlates premiums with risk will reduce moral hazard by diminishing the subsidy from safe to risky institutions.

Least-Cost Resolution

FDICIA requires the FDIC to resolve failed or failing institutions using the method least costly to the insurance fund. This rule of least-cost resolution reduces moral hazard by curtailing the implicit protection too-big-to-fail policies provided to a large depository institution's uninsured depositors, nondepositor creditors, and stockholders, and thereby increases those stakeholders' incentive to monitor and discipline the institution's risk-taking.

THE CULTURE OF AD HOC DISCRETION

Most people would agree that we cannot eliminate discretion and judgment from our current regulatory system. I am certainly not suggesting that we should. But the culture of ad hoc discretion goes beyond that by attacking any statutory rules that limit regulators' flexibility in dealing with weak institutions. It says, "We can handle problems through the examination process or cease-and-desist orders. Substantive statutory rules for supervision serve no useful purpose."

Carried to its logical conclusion, the culture of ad hoc discretion would reject statutory limits on loans to one borrower, restrictions on transactions with affiliates, limits on insider lending, and even capital standards. After all, one could theoretically deal with all these issues case by case, through the examination process. In practice, critics don't go that far. They tacitly accept the pre-FIRREA status quo, but dismiss FDICIA's reforms out of hand. But it's hard to discern a coherent principle in this—a principle explaining why statutory restrictions on transactions with affiliates are acceptable but statutory dividend restrictions are not.

Roots of the Culture

What, then, underlies the culture of ad hoc discretion? I have identified six related elements. Some are more cogent than others, but none justify a sweeping rejection of FDICIA's reforms.

Failure to recognize inherent shortcomings of ad hoc discretion. First, and most important, critics ignore the perverse incentives the pre-FDICIA system created for regulators (which I discussed earlier). They simply assume that right-thinking regulators will do the right thing. But reliance on ad hoc discretion—far from being benign or neutral—was biased toward granting forbearance and overextending the federal safety net.

General resentment toward legal constraints. Second, critics tap a general dislike of legal constraints, which regulators share with many other Americans—that is, we don't like to be tied down. We feel sufficiently confident of our own motivations and capabilities that we see little need for limits on our freedom of action.

In keeping with this inclination, critics depict statutory rules as hindering—never helping—regulators. Yet rules can help. Negotiation provides a useful analogy. If you were entering into tough negotiations, would you really want unlimited negotiating authority? I think not. Reasonable limits on your authority strengthen your bargaining position—and save time—by keeping unreasonable options off the table. Likewise, prompt corrective action enables regulators to skip a long debate over whether to do nothing about a capital-deficient institution and focus on the real question: what action should they take to protect the insurance fund? Rules channel discretion by eliminating options that serve no useful purpose and focusing attention on how best to exercise the discretion that remains.

Critics harp on anomalous cases in which rules might produce a harsh or awkward result. For example, some undercapitalized institutions might conceivably recapitalize more rapidly if they could continue paying dividends. But that doesn't mean we'd be better off without the statutory dividend restriction. The ultimate question is not whether the rule has costs, but whether the costs outweigh the benefits.

Kane has drawn an apt analogy to Odysseus and the Sirens—those sea nymphs whose singing lured mariners to destruction.[3] Odysseus survived by plugging his sailors' ears and having himself bound to the mast. Had he accepted the culture of ad hoc discretion, he would have insisted on keeping his options open, saying, "I'm different. I can listen to the Sirens and still pilot my ship," which would be like saying, "I can drink four scotch-and-sodas and still drive my car."

Misguided traditionalism. Third, critics fail to recognize the policy significance of changes in the financial system over the last two decades or so. Before then—in quieter times—the perverse incentives I have described lay dormant. Relying on ad hoc discretion posed little apparent problem. Regulation shielded depository institutions from competition. A deep conservatism imbued owners, managers, and regulators. Small wonder, then, that failures occurred rarely and caused only modest losses.

But times have changed. Depository institutions no longer enjoy a protected franchise. In the wake of deregulation and financial innovation, they confront tough competition from other financial services firms and from each other. The system has more risk and less room for error than in the past. Failures are more frequent and more costly, and inconsistency in supervision or resolution generates considerable concern.

Realistically, we cannot return our financial system to the 1950s. And we should not rely on ad hoc regulatory flexibility that derived its seeming success from conditions now long gone.

Distrust of markets. Fourth, critics, although complaining about over-regulation, distrust the market forces FDICIA seeks to enlist. Depository institution regulation serves as a substitute for the market discipline that would operate in the absence of deposit insurance and the rest of the federal safety net. Key provisions of FDICIA seek to increase market discipline, as I have previously noted. For example, requiring a significantly undercapitalized institution to sell stock or merge facilitates a market test of its viability. Do investors, offered a sufficient stake in the institution, believe that curing its capital deficiency makes economic sense? But critics fear that the market would overreact. They want to keep regulators' options open—at the price of undercutting the rule's beneficial incentive effects.

Reaction against restrictive legislation. Fifth, critics are in part reacting against other restrictive legislation, current and proposed. They correctly note the difficulty of changing outmoded statutes. They also draw on recent arguments against the rigid firewall provisions in some Glass-Steagall reform proposals. Opponents of such provisions contended that existing safeguards were entirely adequate and obviated any need for legislative firewalls. The catch phrase was "supervision, not regulation." Critics have raised the same theme reflexively against FDICIA. Yet, as I've already noted, FDICIA's key reforms seek in part to ameliorate perverse incentives that would otherwise distort or undermine the supervisory process itself.

Concern about compliance costs. Sixth, critics fear the compliance costs of reform. But which way does the cost issue really cut? FDICIA's key deposit insurance reforms are more incentive-oriented than any previous U.S. banking legislation. One can generally control undesirable behavior far more cost effectively by changing the underlying incentives than through detailed rules of conduct. By ameliorating perverse incentives, FDICIA's key reforms should hinder weak institutions from squeezing net interest margins, help maintain prudent credit standards, reduce losses to the FDIC, and allow deposit insurance premiums to be lower than they otherwise would have been—all of which will improve depository institutions' profitability.

Distorting Debate over Implementing FDICIA

Closely examined, the six elements of the culture of ad hoc discretion do not support a blanket attack on limiting regulatory discretion, especially in the case of reforms seeking to ameliorate perverse incentives that promote excessively risky behavior. Yet the culture has distorted the debate over implementing FDICIA. It has impeded understanding of what is most important in FDICIA and what is not—for example, mischaracterizing the noncapital trip wires, rather than prompt corrective action, as the legislation's defining provisions. It has exacerbated the bitter attacks on FDICIA by regulators and bankers. It has encouraged regulators to pull their punches in interpreting and implementing FDICIA. The resulting minimalism is hardly appropriate for reforms aimed at ameliorating perverse incentives.

Above all, it's an error simply to equate limits on regulatory discretion with an increase in regulatory burden.

NOTES

1. For a detailed discussion of how FDICIA seeks to ameliorate perverse incentives, see Richard Scott Carnell, "A Partial Antidote to Perverse Incen-

tives: The FDIC Improvement Act of 1991," *Annual Review of Banking Law,* vol. 12 (1993), pp. 317–71.

2. Edward J. Kane, *The S&L Insurance Mess: How Did It Happen?* (Washington: Urban Institute, 1989), pp. 20, 103, 128.

3. Edward J. Kane, *The Gathering Crisis in Federal Deposit Insurance* (MIT Press, 1985), p. 162.

RICHARD C. ASPINWALL

Comments

The observations to follow are devoted chiefly to responses by banks to FDICIA during the past year. As a starting point, a distinction must be made between the effects of the economic environment and those of FDICIA itself on bank actions.

On the economic front, the first and one of the foremost forces has been disinflation. Between 1973 and 1981 the consumer price index rose at an average annual rate of about 9½ percent. For the period 1982 to 1991 that average fell to 3½ percent. Many financial decisions made during the 1980s were based on the expectation of a resurgence in the rate of inflation. It is obvious that a substantial amount of expected cash flow never materialized. Moreover, tax legislation in 1986 caused cash flow shortfalls to worsen, reducing after-tax returns on real estate projects—to say nothing of returns on credit to many of those projects.

Second, loan problems at banks soared over the past decade, reflecting the consequences of unsustainable real estate expansion, the excesses of less developed countries, and the legacies of greater balance-sheet leverage by many businesses.

Third, between 1987 and 1992 defense spending fell about 10 percent in real terms. Regional adjustment problems have been especially pronounced in the Northeast and in California.

Fourth, rising fiscal deficits appear to have inhibited the easing of interest rates by the Federal Reserve during periods of weak activity, notably that beginning in the late 1980s.

These are elements of bad news. Nevertheless, there also has been some good news from the economic front. Specifically, two developments have benefited bank efforts to restructure their positions. The foremost is the decline and the steepening of the yield curve. In fourth-quarter 1990 the ninety-one-day Treasury bill rate was 7.21 percent; in fourth-quarter 1992, 3.15 percent—a decline of 406 basis points over the two years. Declines of 276 basis points in the three-year Treasury, to 5.00 percent, and 160 in the ten-year Treasury, to 6.80 percent, were also registered over this period. Accordingly, the spread between the three-month and ten-year Treasury increased from 119 basis points in fourth-quarter 1990 to 365 basis points in fourth-quarter 1992. For 1992 overall this spread averaged 350 basis points, the largest annual spread since the ten-year issue was introduced in 1953. A substantial portion of the 1992 improvement in bank earnings—return on assets averaged almost 100 basis points, twice the average of the previous three years— reflects spread effects.

A second development has been balance sheet restructuring by business and consumers, characterized by debt retirement, maturity extension, and, for consumers, debt consolidation using lower-cost residential mortgage credit. The net result has been weak demand for bank loans, which has facilitated downsizing by banks as a means to attain their preferred capital positions.

In addition to adverse economic developments, banks have faced serious pressures from other sources. The first, and in many ways most fundamental, has been further declines in communications and information processing costs. The fall in these costs has increased the contestability of markets served by banks virtually across the spectrum of bank services. The substitution capabilities of competitors or prospective competitors have been enhanced, especially for vehicles that are substitutes for bank deposits. In addition, access to credit information, previously distinctive to banks, has been achieved by others.

Once users of financial services perfect substitutes for those offered by intermediaries, it is difficult to reverse the process. The growing acceptability of service delivery that does not entail physical proximity erodes one of the distinctive features of banks—the availability of convenient branches. Indeed, so-called no-teller transactions, which account for almost one-third of branch transactions, are being promoted by banks as a means of enhancing operating efficiency. Competitive vulnerability may be an unexpected by-product.

A second form of pressure imposed on banks is a frequent lack of business and market diversification. Some of this stems from inhibitions on branching, some on product array, especially constraints on securities underwriting and distribution and mutual fund operation.

Third, the process of regulatory liberalization of bank powers has been belatedly responsive, never anticipatory. Examples include deposit deregulation, fostered by high interest rates and the growing accessibility of substitutes; broader real estate powers, especially for

S&Ls, intended to overcome interest-rate risk at exactly the time when interest rate movements were becoming more beneficial and real estate disinflation more adverse; and the incremental approach to securities powers under Section 20.

Fourth, Congress was, is, and undoubtedly always will be, averse to mandating changes in market shares. By and large, regulators tend to follow congressional preferences in these matters.

A fifth form of pressure is the imposition of cleanup costs on conservative, well-capitalized banks after the fact. That is, coinsurance costs have been imposed to make up for the losses of those having failed. In addition, FDICIA makes a "systemic-risk exception" to the requirement of least-cost resolution. Any loss resulting to the deposit insurance fund must be recovered through a special assessment on banks.

Changes fostered so far by FDICIA itself stem from the central role of bank capital. As detailed elsewhere in this volume, the act provided for capital ratios and categories, delegating to regulatory agencies matters of definition. The five categories are well capitalized, adequately capitalized, undercapitalized, significantly undercapitalized, and critically undercapitalized. The well-capitalized segment requires that three ratios be met: total risk-based capital greater than 10 percent; tier 1 capital greater than 6 percent of risk-weighted assets; and leverage (tier 1 capital to total average assets) greater than 5 percent.

"Well capitalized" has become an apparent minimum acceptable standard for most banks. Indeed, as Kenneth Scott shows in his paper (table 2), 78 percent of bank assets as of September 1992 were held by well-capitalized banks. There are two main reasons for this preference. First, banks are averse to the increasing operating constraints imposed as capital ratios fall—especially those relating to deposit pricing. Second, bank customers have become much more sensitive to bank conditions. The promulgation of the Financial Accounting Standards Board's (FASB) fair value disclosure requirement will enhance this sensitivity.

Banks actions during 1992 to improve capital positions can be classed along three lines. First is size containment. Over the past year, assets rose 2 percent; loans fell 1½ percent; and deposits were flat, with checkables plus savings rising 15 percent and Cds (large and small) falling 17 percent. The loan figures reflect a substantial volume of securitization, mostly consumer and real estate credit, as well as loan sales outright.

Second, at the same time aggregate size was contained, equity capital expanded materially. Retained earnings and equity flotations added about $27 billion in all to book equity, or 11 percent of equity at yearend 1991. Cash dividend rates were lower than in 1991. Given these developments, the nominal ratio of equity to assets rose to almost 7½ percent, the highest since 1966. In light of shortcomings in the book valuation process, however, this result cannot be viewed without reservation.

Third, in addition to capital additions and the size containment of banks, banks have taken steps to be less intensive users of capital. This has meant a greater emphasis on services that do not explicitly require balance sheet positioning. These include loan originations for sale and a variety of fiduciary, consultative, and back-office processing services. A second capital-relief step is the shift of consumer bank deposits, encouraged by bank pricing, into mutual funds and other investment vehicles, with some of the former managed by banks. Banks face a significant risk, however, that the loss of intermediate- and longer-term consumer deposits to mutual funds will prove difficult to recapture.

In conclusion, FDICIA has increased discipline on banks and on regulators. The degree of rigor involved is not yet assessible, however, because regulatory discretion remains and because new valuation adversity has not yet been experienced. FDICIA has prompted banks to raise new capital by, in effect, making "well capitalized" the preferred standard. Bank sensitivity to the disciplines of market valuations has begun to increase, even though market valuation techniques are not widely incorporated in accounting procedures. Indeed, the effects of the market valuation disclosure mandated by FASB 107 on bank managements should begin to be observable relatively soon—perhaps even before the actions required by FDICIA are all in place.

ANTHONY DOWNS

Comments

I have been asked to discuss FDICIA's effects from the perspective of the real estate development and ownership and management industries. Sadly, the development industry has died from severe indigestion, caused by overeating in the 1980s. All former developers have either been resurrected as asset managers or are still buried. You may know that real estate developers are not the most popular people in the world. Therefore, we bury them fifty feet underground. Why? Because deep down, they are good people. This means that only the ownership and management industries are left in the real estate operations business.

Most of my remarks focus on the aspects of the current credit crunch that go beyond those attributable to FDICIA. I believe FDICIA has played only a minor role in real estate markets and the real estate industry up to now. Consequently, I can ignore the stated subject of this conference and talk about what I prefer.

The credit crunch in lending in commercial real estate officially began in February 1990, when the comptroller of the currency essentially directed banks to stop making any more real estate loans. The basic cause of this credit crunch was the high default rate from overbuilding in the boom of the 1980s. Its roots were stupidity and greed among lenders and developers who expanded into markets clearly containing too much space. That problem was not caused by federal authorities, though their behavior contributed to it.

Also, contrary to many views, lack of accurate information about real estate markets was not a key cause of overbuilding and excessive lending. The office vacancy rate, as reported by Coldwell Banker, in easily available data, rose from 4 percent in 1981 to 20 percent in 1985. It has remained over 19 percent in every quarter since then. Certainly by 1987 any idiot should have realized that almost all office markets were overbuilt. Yet few officials in financial institutions modified their optimistic lending behavior.

This proves to me that banks are run not by just any idiots, but by outstanding idiots. In addition, institutional investors in general—not limited to bankers—are not rational decision makers, contrary to economic theory. Rather, they are group followers like lemmings. That is not a joke but a serious scientific observation that I believe correctly expresses their capabilities and proclivities.

Federal regulators were also slow to recognize the implications of overbuilding. Federal deregulation of banks and thrifts, plus the Tax Act of 1981, partly caused the excessive investment in real estate in the 1980s.

So both the financial lending and investment communities generally, as well as real estate developers and regulators, were amazingly insensitive to clear and readily available evidence about what was actually going on around them.

That reminds me of the story about the bank lending officer and the regulator who were out hunting in the winter in the woods. They came across some tracks in the snow. They began arguing about what kind of tracks these were. The bank regulator said, "I think these are moose tracks." The bank lending officer said, "I think they are deer tracks." They were still standing there arguing when the train hit them.

I believe these observations strongly support the use of rules and regulations to limit the discretion of both regulators and bankers. Based upon extensive past experience, just relying on their abilities and competence to arrive at sound results is totally unrealistic.

In 1990 regulators began putting four pressures on bankers—first, not to make any more real estate loans, regardless of the quality of the loans, or of past relationships with the borrowers, or of whether the borrowers had ever had any defaults or had always paid their loans on time; second, to reduce their total holdings of real estate assets; third, to write down severely the values of nearly all such assets on their books; and fourth, to classify as nonperforming all loans for which market values, as estimated by the regulators, were below the loan amounts on the books, even though the loans were not delinquent in any way.

This situation was aggravated by pressure on bankers from both the stock market and credit-rating agencies. As referred to by other contributors, the stock prices and credit ratings of banks and insurance companies with high percentages of commercial real estate assets were hammered downward. So both these types of institutions stopped making any more real estate loans. Essentially, everybody who had an interest in what banks were doing finally decided that the only way to get banks to stop making bad real estate loans was to hit them over the head.

Two other key factors have contributed to the real estate credit crunch. One consists of recently adopted risk-based-capital requirements; the other is the U.S. Treasury's needs for deficit financing. As other papers mention, these factors have allocated capital away from any private uses exhibiting the slightest degree of risk toward financing our federal deficit. I think this has notably slowed our economic recovery.

The credit crunch in real estate has had several significant impacts, not all of which are fully recognized by the financial community. But most of them appeared before FDICIA was adopted and certainly before it has had any direct effects. Therefore, these effects cannot be fairly blamed on FDICIA itself.

First, two forces—zealous regulators and pressure from investors— have caused commercial real estate prices to fall, I believe, even more than they should have because of basic overbuilding in the 1980s. True, there can be no doubt that overbuilding—not the behavior of regulators—was the major cause of the decline in prices in commercial real estate. But the ending of providing any credit on existing commercial properties aggravated the decline in property prices and values by removing almost all potential buyers from the market.

Markets for all long-term assets need liquidity to function normally. Therefore, when credit vanishes from such a market, as it has, so do possible buyers. Then even a few distressed sellers overbalance the market with more sellers than buyers, driving prices downward. Many financial institutions were eager to unload the real estate that they had acquired through foreclosure, so the market had a lot of distressed sellers but very few buyers.

One of the things that most people do not realize is that the level of prices in any market is not just a reflection of the earning power of the assets concerned, but also of the ratio of sellers and buyers in that market at any particular moment, as expressed in the rate of transactions therein. That is why, for example, real estate prices in the Tokyo office space market were so high. There were a lot of buyers but almost no sellers because Japanese laws and customs encourage investors to hold onto such properties rather than sell them.

Now we have the opposite situation in the United States: there are a lot more sellers than buyers. This has driven the prices of even good quality, still profitable real estate lower than those prices would have been solely because of the deterioration of the market. Owners of sound existing properties, needing refinancing, could not find any lenders willing to put up money. So in many cases, those owners were forced to sell or default. Bankers have become totally hostile to spending money on real estate and much more inclined to spend it on Treasury securities, as has been mentioned.

A second major effect of this situation has been a transformation of the true ownership of most leveraged commercial real estate. Its original developers or subsequent owners have had their initial equities wiped out. That happened because of a price decline of about 25 to 40 percent across the board in all commercial properties in the United States, and 50 percent in office space and many hotels. Therefore, lenders have become the true owners of most commercial properties, even if they have left those properties legally in the hands of the original borrowers. Because the lenders have not always assumed legal ownership, they have not always realized that they have become the true owners of these properties. Therefore, there ought to be a new category on bank books, not just "real estate owned" but "real estate *really* owned." The amount of "real estate *really* owned" is a lot greater than the $28 billion of "real estate owned" now on banks' books.

A third major effect of the credit crunch has been that financial institutions, as a group, cannot sell off their real estate assets nearly as fast as in the past. In fact, they will have to hold most such assets for several years, even though they do not want to. Banks still have about $340 billion in commercial real estate loans, including both development and construction loans, plus more than $28 billion in real estate owned through foreclosures. They would like to get rid of those assets by having somebody else take them out of their ownership. But no one is there to do that. No sources of funds have either enough capital to take over these assets or any desire to do so; at least, not at the current bank book prices or even at substantial discounts from those book values. So banks and insurance companies are going to have to hold these real estate assets for many more years than they originally anticipated.

It is true that every bank chief executive officer wants to unload as many of these real estate assets as he possibly can, as fast as possible. Some banks, like First Chicago, have announced programs to do just that. But it is impossible for *all* banks, or even a great many of them as a group, to unload their properties soon because there is no one to buy those properties. If they all try it at once, commercial real estate prices would be driven down even much lower than they have fallen up to now—far lower than the sellers expected.

Telling all bankers to get rid of their commercial real estate assets is like someone whispering to each person in a room, "If this building catches on fire, in order to be saved, you must be the first person out the door." It sounds like very reasonable advice to each person, but collectively it is impossible.

So the question is, how long can bankers stand to hold onto these properties? And the answer is they are going to have to hold onto them for a long time. Moreover financial institutions have two strong motives for doing so. First, if future market conditions improve, they might obtain higher prices when they sell in a few years than they would now. Therefore, they would sustain smaller capital losses by selling later. That has happened in all previous real estate cycles. Unfortunately, I believe that the increase in real estate prices in this cycle is going to be much slower, if it appears at all, than it was in the 1970s and 1980s.

But even if commercial property prices do not rise in the future, banks are making record profits now, as has been amply described, from the spread between their cost of funds and the interest they obtain on loans. They are building up capital as time passes from these profits. So they can better sustain big losses on real estate in the future than they can now. They could absorb those future losses without taking any real hits against their capital by cushioning the losses with profits set aside over the next few years.

Some bankers claim that regulators have already forced them to write down their real estate assets to liquidation values. Therefore, why should they not sell those real estate assets right now and avoid all the pains of managing them? My answer is if all or even most banks tried to sell off all the real estate assets they want to dispose of right now, including those they really own but have not yet taken over, prices of such properties would be driven even much lower than they are now. Their equity capital losses would then be much larger than now predicted. The banking system could not really sustain equity capital losses of that magnitude.

A fourth implication of the credit crunch is that financial institutions must change their attitudes toward the management of real estate assets they are holding. They need to start acting like responsible owners, not like caretakers burning to sell at the first possible moment. The traditional attitude of a banker toward real estate owned is, "Let's get it out of here as fast as possible; we won't bother to try to manage it well; we will just get rid of it." That is no longer possible. This situation requires a major behavioral change on the part of bankers. Yet it is necessary because the earning power of real estate assets can deteriorate rapidly if they are not aggressively managed, with great attention to detail.

In 1990, a banker went to see a fortune-teller. He said to the fortune-teller, "How long am I going to have to put up with these terrible real estate assets I have on my books?" The fortune-teller looked into her crystal ball and said, "These real estate assets are going to make you terribly poor and unhappy until 1993." He asked, "What will happen after 1993?" She said, "You will get used to it."

What does all of this analysis imply about the impact of FDICIA on commercial real estate markets? Paradoxically, I believe FDICIA has not had much impact on those markets up to now. The major forces driving prices down and restructuring true property ownership predated FDICIA. True, FDICIA's hostility toward real estate lending reinforced the reluctance of banks to make real estate loans. That may have worsened the credit crunch to some extent. But the main factor causing that credit crunch to be more severe than it should have been from pure market forces has been the hostility of regulators toward all types of real estate loans and toward bankers in general.

The anti–real estate zeal of regulators in the field has gone far beyond the directives issued by their top-level superiors. Field regulators have been led by the legendary twenty-eight-year-old MBA who is a veteran of Texas bank failures, and who loves to exhibit his power over much more senior bank CEOs. My friends in banking call him and his kind "the regulators from hell."

Congress bears much of the blame for the excessive zeal of these regulators. Its members threatened to call them before congressional committees on television and berate them for exhibiting too much leniency if they didn't slash real estate property values on banks' books. Naturally, the regulators did not want to go through that humiliating experience.

I think risk-based-reserve requirements also deserve some of the blame for banks' excessively anti-real-estate-lending behavior. Those requirements create strong incentives for bankers to put funds into Treasury securities rather than any type of risky private-sector loans.

Even without any of these factors, commercial real estate prices certainly would have fallen a great deal simply because of overbuilding. But the net result of all these additional factors has been lower prices than would otherwise have occurred, plus bigger bank capital write-offs than would have been necessary with more prudent policies. However, neither of these results is the fault of FDICIA. Whether FDICIA's immense reregulation of banks will cause further problems in real estate markets remains to be seen. I leave that to the banking experts to argue about, as they certainly have today.

Meanwhile, federal authorities need to provide more pressure on banks to accommodate reasonable loan requests on existing real estate and other forms of activity. If FDICIA's extensive regulations help restore banks' willingness to take at least some risks, then FDICIA will have been worthwhile in spite of the undoubtedly high cost of operating under so many detailed regulations.

It is interesting to me that, at the president-elect's economic summit in Arkansas in late 1992, some banker said that a 4 percent increase in total bank loans would generate more than an $80 billion increase in spending in the economy. He said that would have a much greater positive effect than the stimulus policies of the federal government that were being discussed at that meeting. In a similar vein, Congressman Leach says in his comments that the biggest problem in banking today is the role of banks in strengthening the economy, not the role of the economy in strengthening the banks.

Where To From Here?

BARBARA TIMMER

Deposit Insurance: Back to the Future

In my opinion, this has been a substantive conference. My paper was shortened because of the incredible expertise of the other participants. That is a testimony not only to the people involved but, to my belief, that we have been very fortunate in being able to work together on probably one of the biggest economic issues in our lifetime. I consider myself very fortunate to have been involved in the series of crises that make up the collapse of the deposit insurance funds. I think it has been a wonderful experience.

I want to cite a GAO report, entitled "Insurer Failures: Regulators Failed To Respond in Timely and Forceful Manner in Four Large Life Insurer Failures," the language of which is similar to preceding papers in this volume. GAO is testifying on its finding about the failures of four large insurance companies and the effectiveness of state solvency regulation of these insurers. "The four insurers failed, in large part, because of reckless practices, poorly controlled growth, and risky high yield investments during the 1980s. The four insurers relied on questionable reinsurance transactions to artificially inflate their surpluses. The four failed insurers had significant internal control weaknesses over their investment activities, reinsurance arrangements, insurance sales practices, and transactions with affiliates. California and New York regulators had evidence for years before the takeovers that the insurers were insolvent. However, regulators failed to respond to danger signals and did not take timely or forceful action to avert the failures or minimize policy holder losses. Statutory accounting and reporting requirements prescribed by regulators failed to insure the filing of financial statements that presented the true magnitude of the deterioration. Interaffiliate transactions were a regulatory blindspot. Upon finding solvency problems, California and New York regulators initially chose to forbear, rather than promptly disclose the insurers' true condition. GAO believes new authority must include requirements compelling regulators to intervene when insurers operate in hazardous conditions, characteristic of failure."

David Mullins's speech that he gives about government-sponsored enterprises and the layers of government subsidized and implicitly guaranteed debt spells out the problems in our future. That whole wave is out there, and the truth is that the amount of pieces of debt paper—and in this age of technology you don't even really need paper—and the promises to pay debt in all their forms and in all their manifestations are staggering. I think what we have done with the deposit insurance funds and the collateral that collapsed underneath them, the asset management and disposition skills we have learned, will be the expertise to take into these new fields.

We complained about bank accounting requirements and not knowing the true condition of insured depository institutions. Some of these other entities have similar problems. Last week I had dinner with a lawyer friend of mine in San Diego. First he did work for the bank board, then he did FDIC and RTC work. He said that he is excited to be moving into a new field. He finally has great contracts out there ready to go with the insurance companies.

So where are we headed? Bigger and maybe better, although I am not sure about the better.

Getting back to my first theme, which is a farewell of sorts to the deposit insurance system, as we knew it, I can remember a conference on these issues in 1989. At the end of the conference, John Anderson spoke, representing a major metropolitan newspaper. We were hearing, really, for the first time, the depth of the problems in the deposit insurance funds and what needed to be done.

At the end of the day, the room was in a state of seated collapse. John Anderson stood up and said, "Boy, I will tell you one thing. At least, this has proved that deposit insurance has worked."

I can remember thinking about that, and the moderator, sitting next to me, stood up and said, "Just a minute. Excuse me, I would like to interrupt. That sounds to me like a guy who gets up in the morning, goes to his garage, backs his Porsche out, runs full tilt into the wall, crashing the car, the airbag pops out, and he says, 'Well, the airbag worked.'" Of course, you can't drive the car.

That was the sense I had back then. It seems like ten years ago. It is probably two or three. Really, the system of deposit insurance had collapsed; and in fact it worked as long as we didn't need it.

To me a very seminal report on this whole issue was the Congressional Budget Office report done for my former chairman, which basically stated that insured depository institutions ran into two problems:

One, competition in all kinds of forms and interest rates, and all the noninsured depository institutions doing the same kinds of things; and, two, a regulatory collapse. The report also said that those were catastrophes, that the insurance fund was designed to deal with single failures, not catastrophes.

In my opinion, it was also designed to pay for the regulatory structure. Basically, we had, instead of single failures, a collapse.

I think this volume contains all the possible reasons for why the deposit insurance funds collapsed. I think, frankly, that almost all of them have some truth, but that it is a multifaceted collapse.

When I say I feel fortunate to have seen the collapse, it has been very interesting. I date the beginning of the collapse to March 27, 1980, which is the date that silver prices collapsed. Thinking back into the late 1970s with the high interest rates, there were people who were saving beans in their basement and talking about paper currency and hard money.

I remember the Hunt brothers coming and testifying in front of my old subcommittee and talking about the only real investments being oil and gas and things you could touch and feel—that included silver. I think, really in some ways, that was the first speculative bubble that collapsed, the first speculative bubble caused by inflationary thinking.

I have followed silver prices ever since. I did a graph of silver prices for a report I did for Ben Rosenthal. It went along a very straight line for years and years and years. I did a 100-year graph, and it took about ninety years for silver to get to $6, then it went up to $52, and then came back down again. It was back at $6. Silver is now at less than $4.

Because silver has some precious metal qualities and some industrial qualities, it was an interesting price to follow. It is now lower than it was literally four decades earlier. I have seen this rolling collapse. I guess we have all seen that coming through the system.

Real estate hit insured depository institutions particularly hard because that was the underlying collateral that a lot of institutions depended on.

I am not the first to say this, but I think there is another collapse coming. I heard someone on "Wall Street Week in Review," far more articulately than I could, describe what he thought was the coming collapse of debt paper: Bonds and maybe ultimately Treasury securities.

How much debt can we repay? Really, when I say "speculative

bubble," we have lived through a time period when we have had to shift our thinking about how things always work. Someone was talking about the consumer price index (CPI). We thought it was always going to be one direction on the graph, and it turns out that maybe that is not accurate.

I didn't get a chance to see all the Ross Perot infomercials, but I have my own multipurpose chart. As the chart shows, the value of real estate collateral can be seen in one of two ways. You can hold onto that property, waiting for it to come back. Or, as a friend of mine pointed out years ago, you can continue to eat the holding costs because it will never come back. Being with the FSLIC meant getting a chance to learn about holding costs for four years.

The lawyers gradually realized that, when the property managers came in with a plan and told you what they thought the holding costs were going to be, so they could fix it up before they sold it, you should multiply the holding costs by two. That is how the lawyers figured out the real holding costs.

Somebody pointed out in a previous paper that banks have got to decide whether to sit and hope or sell. That hope, I think, proves that deep at heart, no matter where we are from, we are all religious; and even though we are not all from the Midwest, that hopeful aura from Ohio and Michigan has permeated even to Wall Street, even to the urban centers where the banks hold on to real estate.

FDICIA—to me you can't really talk about FDICIA without talking about FIRREA. In a sense, those two bills apply very similar structures to very similar collapses in the two insurance funds.

There were several forms of moral hazard. Regulators couldn't be tough; bankers didn't have anything to lose; so we took away some of the regulators' discretion and tried to cover less of the deposits. We tried to put more of the bankers' capital at risk. And, frankly, that almost sums up those two bills.

I think, personally, the use of capital restoration plans for institutions that fall below minimum capital so that you get to have a personal relationship with your primary regulator in a structured way was very important.

In my new job, I met over the phone last night the general counsel for—it turns out, unbeknownst to me, that my new company owns an insured depository institution—our savings bank, which is in California. So during the phone conversation last night he said, "What did you do?" I said, "Well, I used to be general counsel for the House Banking Committee." There was a pause. He said, "Are you responsible for FIRREA?" I said, "What part of FIRREA are you thinking about? Maybe it is that Senate part that you don't like. Mainly, I was in charge of making sure that the cross references worked." He said, "Oh, yes, most of them do; don't they?"

I have to say, listening to Richard Scott Carnell give what I thought was a very good presentation, that I really respect the amount of thinking that went into his presentation. It is an honor to have worked with some of the participants in the conference, like him, on this statutory language.

The truth is we worked very hard together to put into technically accurate language good public policy—and the policies represented in FIRREA and FDICIA are the policies of the elected members of the House and Senate representing their constituents. If you saw the mail about the "taxpayer bailout" that the members receive, you would realize that these bills got passed because that was what people thought needed to happen.

I know it has been a painful process, but I think, in a sense, everyone who worked on this can be proud. I think the people who have come in from banks and from the private sector, and who have argued with the provisions have all been helpful; every argument makes for a better product.

The reason I know that we are at the end of an era is this: Last night, David Letterman came up with ten reasons why we know we are at the end of the collapse of the insurance deposit funds.

"Number 10: The incoming president understands the issue.

"Number 9: Nobody is planning to introduce comprehensive legislation.

"Number 8: All the studies mandated in FIRREA are done.

"Number 7: No one who voted for FIRREA is left on the Banking Committee.

"Number 6: Every network has had a special.

"Number 5: The real estate guy at Brookings has a bigger joke repertoire than Jay Leno.

"Number 4: There is only one scheduled conference on FDICIA left.

"Number 3: There are hardly any banks left.

"Number 2: Bob Litan is using the collapse of the insurance deposit funds as a springboard for a new job.

"Number 1: We all know each other by first name; we don't even need nametags."

With that, I would like to say, in a sense, farewell myself. I think that the people on the House Banking Committee staff—and sometimes some of the staff from the other committees—helped to make the language as technically accurate as possible. I think the agencies have worked diligently trying to implement what they thought was not only the intent of the legislation but what was best for insured depository institutions.

I know I am biased but I think the lawyers at the law firms that have gradually come to learn a very complicated set of issues on behalf of their clients have done excellent jobs.

I think the press has become educated. I think there have been some excellent books written. In my opinion you should read them all. Every time I see Martin Mayer, I think about having every one of his books.

I think about the members of Congress—the House and Senate— who had to publicly vote on these issues, these most unpopular issues (which is why we tried to make them bipartisan). They have really had to take courageous stands.

I thank all the people who did not participate in the conference, the people who are out in the field still working. I remember when I was at the bank board, being on the road and trying to work—in essence, I think we felt we were all working night and day, trying to manage this contraction. I think all of them deserve thanks.

The person I ended up thinking about, who could not participate and who I know would have, is Bill Taylor. I want to dedicate my remarks to him. He and I first met when we worked together on the collapse of the silver markets and we stayed friends for all that time. I felt that he was the essence, really, of a dedicated public servant. To me he represented something that we could all strive for in our work and particularly in our work in a crisis like this, where our decisions have such effect on people.

ROBERT E. LITAN

Some Thoughts on the Future of Banking "Reform"

The election of Bill Clinton to the presidency marks a dividing line between the old and the new banking agendas. The old agenda, or the one that has preoccupied Congress and the administration for the past twelve years, has centered on ensuring safety and soundness and on restructuring the financial services industry—namely interstate banking and broader powers for banks or their holding companies. The new agenda that Bill Clinton brings to town will focus instead on regulatory relief and establishing a network of community development banks (CDBs).

First I consider the old agenda, and specifically the restructuring proposals of the Bush administration that did not find their way into the 1991 banking reform legislation. Is there any prospect that this part of the old agenda will be acted on in the near future? I have my doubts. Despite the optimism expressed in some quarters that the Clinton administration will endorse interstate banking, I do not see why the stalemate that prevented the adoption of interstate banking and branching in 1991—specifically, the refusal of the large banks to accept restrictions on the interstate sale of insurance as the price for geographic banking freedom—will be broken anytime in the near future. I don't detect a shift among banks; nor do I see any evidence that insurance agents will back off their efforts to preclude banks from exporting their state-authorized insurance powers.

Similarly, I see little enthusiasm in the new administration and in Congress for authorizing broader powers for bank holding companies. I am nevertheless encouraged by the warm words William Haraf has for the narrow bank concept as the vehicle for extending broader powers to bank holding companies. Still, however, the narrow bank proposal is a long way from adoption.

The fact remains that Congress legislates in the banking area only in response to a current crisis (a tendency that describes congressional action in most areas). What kind of crisis would it take for Congress to actually move on structural reform?

Richard Aspinwall may unintentionally answer the question in his comments when he says that his bank and others have been studying the option of giving up the charter. If one or two very large money center banks actually did this, perhaps that would trigger Congress to say, "If we have so completely tied up the industry that the best banks are leaving the system, and thereby leaving the FDIC with banks of lesser safety, then maybe we (Congress) should do more to keep banks from dropping their charters by giving the industry nationwide interstate authority and broader powers for its holding companies."

What about the safety and soundness portion of the old banking agenda? There is not much more to be done, in my view, given the enactment of capital-based early intervention in FDICIA, which I endorse.

Should anything else be done? Lee Hoskins suggests in his paper that politically based systems of bank discipline are inherently less desirable than market-based methods. Accordingly, he and others call for the scaling back or even elimination of federal deposit insurance.

I agree with Hoskins that more market discipline would be useful, but depositors are not the only source of such discipline. As several other commentators have noted in this volume, holders of subordinated debt can prevent banks from taking excessive risk. Unlike depositors, who can run from their banks if they fear them about to topple, sub debt holders cannot run and therefore provide a much more stable source of discipline.

For this reason, I would urge the new administration to require all large banks—say, those with assets over $5 billion—to meet their tier 2 capital requirement with some minimum portion of subordinated debt. Under such a system, large banks would be able to grow only by convincing the market to purchase new issues of sub debt.

I now want to turn to the new Clinton agenda, and specifically to the issue of regulatory relief. For many, this translates into doing something about the so-called credit crunch.

There is a clear divergence of views on this topic. David Mullins says in his paper that he had doubts about the existence of such a crunch—in the sense that banks are not making loans to willing borrowers—

except with respect to small businesses, whom Mullins believes may have been discouraged from borrowing by excessively stringent bank examination standards. A much different view was expressed at the economic conference in Little Rock, however, by the president of the American Bankers Association, who was much more aggressive in blaming bank regulation for discouraging banks from lending.

Is there any way to reconcile these views? I suggest that there is and it lies in my belief that there is a crunch, but that it is regional rather than national. If one looks between the coasts, by and large, the banks are well off, and there hasn't been a real estate collapse. If the banks in these states are not making loans, it is because nobody wants to borrow.

I can perhaps best illustrate this by reporting the following anecdote. My father, who still lives in my hometown of Wichita, Kansas, recently told me about Fourth National Bank in Wichita, the largest bank in the city, which was so desperate for loans that it was offering lottery tickets to borrowers of $1,000 or more. That is how desperate the banks were for loans.

Fourth National is probably typical of most banks between the coasts, but not so of the banks on the East Coast or in southern California, where significant declines in commercial real estate prices have eroded bank capital positions, and therefore bank lending capacity. In those regions of the country, the decline in bank lending is not simply due to a lack of demand, but also to a constriction of supply.

Again, another anecdote helps illustrate the point. In the summer of 1992, the Bank of Boston intensively advertised the fact that it was willing to make available up to $3 billion in loans to small businesses. The bank was soon avalanched with requests for loans. To be sure, a lot of the requests came from noncreditworthy companies. But many were quite meritorious, and I believe that the bank had in fact loaned about $1 billion. The conclusion I draw from the Bank of Boston's experience is that, unlike in the Midwest, there is a demand for credit in the Northeast that is not being fully met, because banks there have either been unwilling or unable to satisfy it.

Moreover, even Mullins concedes that some aspects of current bank regulatory policy may be constraining bank lending. For example, he notes that under the risk weightings of the Basle bank capital accord, banks face roughly a fifty-basis-point penalty, relative to a plain leverage ratio, in making a conventional loan. In addition, Mullins suggests that bank examiners are applying excessively stringent collateral requirements to small business loans.

As a result, I would expect the Clinton administration to examine both the Basle capital standards, and the documentation and collateral requirements for business lending. The Clinton team may also pay attention to the valuation of nonperforming commercial real estate loans.

As Downs suggests in his remarks, in real estate markets where few buyers can obtain financing but do meet a lot of sellers, the few transactions that take place may occur at distressed prices, which do not properly reflect the long-run value of similar real estate. To put it differently, real estate markets tend to overshoot on the way down as well as on the way up, and thus the use of liquidation prices to value real estate can lead to excessive markdowns of bank capital ratios and, in turn, to excessive restriction on bank lending in regions of the country hit by declining real estate prices, such as the Northeast and mid-Atlantic states and southern California.

To be sure, bank regulators were told by the Bush administration not use liquidation values, but everything I have heard from bankers around the country suggests that bank examiners haven't listened. The Clinton administration will probably try again, but it is not clear at this point whether it will have any greater success.

One final point about regulatory relief. Bankers make some good points when they complain about excessively detailed regulation, such as the 267-page truth-in-lending regulations that Hoskins notes in his paper. I question, however, how much truly meritorious regulatory relief regulators can supply on their own, and how much requires legislation—and specifically, rollbacks of what some may view as the "bank-bashing" elements of FDICIA. If legislation is required to provide the bankers with any real regulatory relief, then it is doubtful that bankers will be satisfied, since the chairmen of both the House and Senate Banking Committees are going to be reluctant to overturn much of what their committees, and Congress as a whole, produced in 1991.

The other key part of the Clinton banking agenda, of course, is the new president's proposal to "clone" South Shore Bank of Chicago and to form a nationwide network of 100 or more community development banks. The main purpose of the proposal would be to help rejuvenate the inner cities by increasing the availability of funds for commercial purposes.

Some might question the need for CDBs, arguing that if there is little lending going on in low-income areas, that is a market outcome reflecting the risks involved. I believe this is too narrow a view, however. Private credit judgments for low-income residents—whether for residential or commercial purposes—do not include the broader social benefits of rejuvenating depressed areas.

If we could truly bring economic progress to some of the inner cities, it is more than likely that we will cut down on a variety of social problems—such as drugs, crime, and malnutrition—which collectively cost society tens of billions of dollars a year.

Although I certainly do not argue that supplying credit and capital to the inner cities is the magic bullet that will solve these social problems, I feel comfortable in asserting that these difficulties cannot be addressed unless the inner cities have businesses that can employ the residents who live there. In turn, the inner cities cannot be rejuvenated unless both credit and capital are made available to private entrepreneurs who do business there.

In principle, CDBs can help realize this objective. Indeed, I believe it is possible that the South Shore Bank model, if it can be replicated, can be *more* successful in channeling credit in a useful manner to the inner cities than can conventional banks by meeting their Community Reinvestment Act (CRA) requirements.

The reason is that CDBs would have only a single mission: to revitalize inner cities. Their staff and officers would be dedicated to this mission and nothing else. That is far different from the situation of an ordinary commercial bank that has a CRA department whose operations are not necessarily integral to the bank's success.

There is a great distance, however, between the theory and practice of community development banking. And what we are likely to witness in 1993 is an effort by the Clinton administration to flesh out the concept. I conclude by listing some of the more important questions that will have to be addressed and some of my tentative answers.

First, how are CDBs to be funded? The Levy Institute has published a paper suggesting that the federal government could do so, perhaps by appropriating funds for a new Federal Community Development Bank, which in turn would make equity investments in individual CDBs.

In an era of huge federal budget deficits, however, the government will be tempted to look for other ways to finance the CDBs. The obvious alternative is to give banks CRA points for investing capital or deposits in CDBs.

Second, what qualifies as a CDB? I believe regulators should be flexible, specifying a menu of qualified institutions, including a conventional deposit-taking bank like South Shore, the roughly 100 credit unions that now serve low-income areas, and community development corporations, which provide equity capital.

Third, given the shortage of people who know how to lend in low-income areas—especially for commercial purposes—how can CDBs be built up without running great risks that many will fail and much money will be wasted? This is perhaps the most important challenge, and I don't pretend to have all the answers now, but several thoughts come to mind.

For one thing, the program should be built up slowly, with a key emphasis on training. My bias, by the way, is that training community activists to be loan officers is likely to be more productive than taking former commercial loan officers and trying to turn them into community lenders. The training will have to be run by the few people in the country expert in this kind of activity, such as those from South Shore and its Arkansas affiliate.

My other key suggestion is that much greater attention be paid to credit unions as a model for the CDB program—not necessarily the only model, but a much more important one than has heretofore been recognized. Because credit unions are mutually owned, the managers have far less incentive to divert loans to favored interests than managers of shareholder-owned banks. In addition, given their nonprofit status, credit unions may be able to provide necessary checking account services at lower cost than banks.

Fourth, will it be necessary to implement the CDB proposal through legislation or can it be done administratively? My short answer to this is that probably much can be done administratively through interpretation of the CRA provisions.

Finally, how should the administration react when the inevitable CDB failure occurs and someone finds that loan monies have been wasted? My answer here is to prepare the nation in advance for what is at stake, perhaps by using an analogy coined by my Brookings mentor, Arthur Okun, who was Lyndon Johnson's chief economic adviser. Okun observed that all government programs have "leaky buckets," such that some portion of the monies put into them are wasted or used for administrative expenses. We're lucky if at the end of the day 80 cents on the dollar is left in the bucket and not 20.

The challenge for CDB enthusiasts is to design a program that will hit the 80 percent target, or something close to it. The fact that it won't hit 100 cents on the dollar—as it inevitably won't—should not matter, because today, for inner-city residents, the credit bucket is about empty.

W. LEE HOSKINS

FDICIA's Regulatory Changes and the Future of the Banking Industry

In 1991 Congress passed the Federal Deposit Insurance Corporation Improvement Act (FDICIA), a statute aimed at protecting the deposit insurance fund and thus taxpayers, via a host of regulations in the banking industry. Is FDICIA a bane or boon for the taxpayer? The answer, I believe, depends on how successful the law is in limiting costs to the taxpayer in the face of the cost of regulation to the economy. It is by no means clear that the statute will successfully limit losses to the taxpayer. It may be that the cost to the economy of a highly regulated banking system will be offset by efficiencies gained through the expansion of the nonbank providers of financial services, but that happy outcome for the economy is certainly not assured. Put differently, the taxpayer may not lose a dollar because of bank failures, but he or she may lose in terms of a less productive and efficient economy as a result of an overregulated banking industry.

Fortunately, my task now is to focus on the future of the banking industry rather than to attempt to answer this question. Although many forces are shaping banking today—increasing competition and changing technology—I focus primarily on the regulatory changes in FDICIA as they affect banking's future. I first discuss why FDICIA is a second-best solution for the taxpayer. Next I examine the strategies banks will consider. One strategy is to continue to lobby for reducing the regulatory burden and achieving fundamental reform. Another is to innovate around the regulatory burden or prepare to sell (or liquidate) the bank. Last, I put forth a few observations about likely outcomes.

SECOND BEST, NOT GOOD ENOUGH

When policymakers and economists propose solutions to economic problems, they all too often fail to make clear whether the solutions are based on economic principles or on politically achievable policy. I suspect many people, including those who provided the intellectual foundation for FDICIA, would recommend a different solution if asked to base their recommendations solely on economic principles. The problem with proposing a second-best solution—the politically achievable one—is that the public may come to believe it is the best solution that economic analysis has to offer. Ultimately, it is public understanding of economic policy that makes good public policy politically achievable. By not clearly stating the preferred solution, we are ensuring that it will never be achieved. The largest cost of FDICIA may well be the delaying or eliminating of the possibility of fundamental reform. In short, the second best, while not good enough, ultimately precludes achieving something better.

Although I have given intellectual support to several of the provisions of FDICIA, I have done so only in the context of more fundamental reforms.[1] The fundamental reform needed is the sharp curtailment of federal deposit insurance. Shifting the risk of loss in financial decisions from the taxpayer to managers who make decisions will better the decisions that are made. Market discipline, not regulation, should determine financial decisionmaking. Let anyone who wants to open a bank do so, but without federal deposit insurance, a central bank discount window, or a government-sponsored payment mechanism that offers daylight overdraft credit. If private entities want to replace the withdrawn federal guarantees, then let them do so at the explicit cost to their users.

Those who support the expanded regulation approach entailed in FDICIA are displaying greater faith in "their regulations" being more effective than the mountain of regulations already on the books. This faith is not supported by the historical record. Loopholes will appear and regulators will forebear. In addition, FDICIA will generate efficiency losses that emanate from the regulations adopted to counter the distorted and perverse incentives at work in the financial system.

Some would argue that these costs are already quite large. The new administration is rumored to be examining the effect of the regulatory burden on bank lending and economic activity. Moreover, bankers have become increasingly aware of the relationship between the safety net and regulations. In an October 1992 survey by the Federal Reserve Bank of Minneapolis, 81 percent of the bank respondents preferred a cutback in deposit insurance and the concomitant market discipline as opposed to FDICIA regulation and supervision.[2]

Neither bankers nor others have focused on an inconsistency in the logic of FDICIA. Since banks are to be closed when they still have a positive net worth, taxpayers are not at risk for loss. Why then does the deposit insurance fund need to be recapitalized by achieving a fund equal to 1.25 percent of insured deposits as soon as practicable, but not longer than fifteen years? Surely if the early closure regulations work, losses to the fund will be nonexistent. Insurance fees should be reduced, not increased. I believe the costs to the economy and to the banking industry associated with FDICIA will prompt remedial legislation; indeed it already has done so. Whether such legislative efforts will be an improvement or hindrance is another matter. And as past experience has demonstrated, it will also prompt "innovation" aimed at escaping regulatory constraints and cost.

WHERE TO FROM HERE?

Bankers are likely to pursue several strategies as a result of FDICIA, none of which are mutually exclusive. One strategy is to work on reforming the regulations and the statute. Another is to change the operation of the bank to reduce the regulatory costs. Still another is to work to reduce the safety net and hence the underlying rationale for the regulations. Yet another may be for bankers to lobby for extension of the regulations (and the safety net) to the nonregulated providers of financial services. But leveling the playing field in that manner is not the way to go. Last, bankers, by accepting the present safety net and FDICIA, will follow what I believe is an implicit strategy of preparing the bank for sale or liquidation.

Efforts are well under way on the first strategy. Many bankers and trade associations have commented on proposed regulations associated with FDICIA. In a few instances, proposed regulations have been revised. In others, bankers have failed. For example, despite dissents by my former colleagues, Governors Larry Lindsey and John LaWare, the Federal Reserve approved a 267-page regulation for the "truth in savings" provision of the act. I am sure this is an important regulation but as a matter of perspective, I am told that the Lord's Prayer has but 56 words, the Ten Commandments, 297 words, and the Declaration of Independence, 300 words. The cost of complying with FDICIA is high—in many cases more than 10 percent of a bank's noninterest expense.[3] And many of the provisions of the act, such as "truth in savings," were not even issues consumers cared much about.

Concerted efforts by bankers and trade associations to change regulations will pay dividends. I make this statement out of the conviction that, at least for now, the marginal benefit from doing so far exceeds the added costs. First, regulations are not statutes, and they can be modified at much less cost to the banking industry. Second, many of the regulations are still in proposal form. Thus regulators do not have a body of previous decisions that they have to overturn to modify a proposed regulation. This fact lowers the perceived cost to the regulator for making modifications. Third, regulators recently have been under attack by their bosses, the politicians, for causing the "credit crunch," a weak economy, and continued distress in the commercial real estate market. Regulators may well see the cost to them as high for not being responsive to charges of "overregulation" in the implementation of FDICIA. The benefit to bankers of limiting the potential regulatory micromanagement of their banks is large and, for some banks, critical to their long-term viability. The incentives for both bankers and regulators point in the same direction.

It seems to me that bankers should strive for capital adequacy–based easements to regulations. Once a bank achieves the "well capitalized" rating, it should have its regulatory burdens substantially reduced. The frequency and comprehensiveness of examinations could be reduced. The application process could be expedited or eliminated. Many reporting requirements could be eliminated. The closer capital requirements bring banks to their nonbank competitors' capital levels, the weaker is the rationale for regulating them at all.

What about the prospects for more fundamental reform? Having spent considerable time over the past five years arguing for a reduced federal safety net and deregulation of the banking industry, I am not optimistic about the near term chances for fundamental reform. A new president and Congress will receive the same conflicting signals from various banking trade associations, other financial service providers, and the folks back home that the Bush administration and Congress received. Real reform is not attainable, in my opinion, until two conditions are met. First, bankers must recognize that the federal safety net is the direct source of much of the regulatory burden. Second, voters need to recognize that federal deposit insurance primarily benefits the wealthy (in 1988, 1.4 percent of American families controlled more than 28 percent of total bank deposits), but imposes a regulatory burden that they ultimately pay for and puts them at risk for increased future tax liabilities. FDICIA codifies the "too big to fail" policy, giving three public officials the legal right to increase future taxes on all Americans. I suspect that before this decade is finished these costs will be much more apparent to all parties. The costs of bad financial policies and practices tend to surface much more quickly in a world of highly integrated capital markets. A new president and Congress must be educated about the cost to the economy (not just to banks) of FDICIA. Fundamental reform that relies on market discipline rather than regulation should be the message.

Another strategy that is well under way is that of "innovating" around the regulatory burden. One aspect of this strategy is to reconsider the issue of a bank charter. For some banks, dropping the bank charter and becoming a nonbank bank may be in the best interest of shareholders. When bank capital levels approach those of the unregulated financial service providers, the value of deposit insurance and the discount window are small. A similar avenue is to explore new types of charters with state legislators, who are disgruntled by the federal usurpation of power under FDICIA. Creative ideas about new types of charters that permit broader powers will find fertile fields in the state regulatory community.

Perhaps the most important innovations will come from the banks' balance sheet, with emphasis on economizing on insured deposit funding and capital. What specific innovations are we likely to see? The answer is unknown, but we can be sure they will come. Every cost-increasing regulation sets in motion a cost-avoidance reaction by banks. The idea is not likely to come from some well-compensated CEO, but rather from some manager in a small profit center struggling to meet his net-income target. It is the thousands of these managers spread across the country who will discover loopholes in the regulations. And that is why regulators can never write a regulation that can foreclose all the ways around it.

I will speculate on a few innovations that seem likely to occur. One is to shift more activities to the holding company, forming a nonlegislated narrow bank in the process. Originating, selling, and servicing assets at the holding company can economize on deposit funding as well as capital. In response to FDICIA, Huntington National Bank compared the profitability of booking indirect auto paper as opposed to securitizing it. In terms of net income, the two alternatives are quite close. If banking companies shift more activities funded by commercial paper to the holding company and shrink the bank, they will have less reason over time to have a bank subsidiary. In short, FDICIA, by raising the price of funding assets with insured deposits, is like passing a tax on the size of windows—over time smaller windows is the result. Of course the obvious area for innovation is to go "off balance sheet" in ways yet to be anticipated. These innovations may actually produce public as well as private gains, but perhaps not. The troubling aspect to me is that all this creative activity is prompted by regulation and not by changes in the economy or markets and that it may end up shifting risk back to the taxpayer through some other implicit or explicit government guarantee, possibly associated with the payment system.

The last strategy I want to mention is the default strategy. To do nothing in response to FDICIA is tantamount to preparing the bank for sale or liquidation. This option will be implicitly exercised by an increasing number of banks. As FDICIA's costs become imbedded in the operation of a bank, and the bank does not respond, then its return on assets and equity will begin to decline. Early on in this process the bank becomes a takeover target. Later it becomes a candidate for regulatory intervention resulting in sale or liquidation.

SOME OBSERVATIONS

Bank earnings are currently very strong and will continue to be strong through most of 1993. These earnings reflect substantial net interest margins that are not likely to prevail in the future as the spread between borrowing and lending rates narrows. In 1994 the full cost of FDICIA to banks will no longer be masked by such strong margins. Banks that act now to alter their operations to reflect the higher costs of booking assets funded with insured deposits will move ahead of the pack in 1994. Those that do not run the risk of becoming targets for other banks or regulators. Over the rest of the decade, banks that actively find ways around the costs of regulation are more likely to be successful not only against bank competitors but also against nonbanks. Such banks will have operating units that resemble their nonbank competitors. They will have selected managers that rely very little on deposit insurance as a substitute for capital. When fundamental reform that relies on market discipline and counterparty scrutiny finally returns to banking, these managers will have a leg up on the competition.

This outcome seems likely to me not because of my strong belief in the efficiency of markets—markets can be made less efficient by a government's actions—but because of the degree of freedom governments have in imposing such actions. I do not believe deregulation of financial markets is occurring around the world because wise men in power believe in the efficacy of markets. Usually wise men in power deregulate because they have little choice. The integration of world financial markets means the world's financial resources are brought to bear on a government's policies or regulatory practices that are inconsistent with wealth-maximizing activities. FDICIA, if left unchanged, will have a lot less of the financial market to regulate by the end of the decade.

NOTES

1. W. Lee Hoskins, "The Need for Reform," The Garn Institute of Finance, Annual Conference, Salt Lake City, February 7, 1991; and "Reforming the Banking and Thrift Industries: Assessing Regulation and Risk," 1989 Frank M. Engle Lecture in Economic Security, The American College, Bryn Mawr, Pa., May 1989.

2. "Opinion Poll," *FedGazette*, vol. 4 (October 1992).

3. Ibid. Of the respondents, 52 percent indicated that FDICIA compliance cost 3–10 percent of noninterest expense; 36 percent of the respondents believed the cost to exceed 10 percent.

General Discussion

BACKGROUND OF THE ACT: INTELLECTUAL AND POLITICAL HISTORY

The conference began with a discussion of why Congress enacted only a portion of the Treasury proposal and failed to adopt the recommendations dealing with interstate banking and broader product powers for banks and bank holding companies. Robert Glauber felt that President Bush did a great deal and the result could not have been any different. As for how the package would fare under the new administration and Congress, Glauber said that the feature most likely to pass is interstate branching.

Franz Oppenheimer had a different view about why much of the Treasury proposal failed to gain passage. The primary reason was that the conclusions and recommendations had no relation to the discussions in the document or to previous studies. Second, the Treasury never faced the analytical dichotomy between universal banking and core banking and tried to bridge it with an inadequate holding company proposal. Finally, the proposal ignored the difficulty of applying the legislative proposals to foreign banks.

Barbara Timmer believed the problem with getting enough votes for the Treasury proposal was the lack of consensus on whether banks should be granted additional insurance and securities powers and the authority to ignore state boundaries. Timmer also discussed the larger economic problems of the 1970s and 1980s, including fluctuations in the interest rate and changes in credit standards and real estate values. She observed that while insured depository institutions reflected these larger problems, many people believed that the institutions helped to cause the economic problems by unwise lending.

Several discussants turned to the topic of Glass-Steagall reform. Douglas Kidd suggested that perhaps the most fundamental mistake made by those dealing with reform politics was in not accepting a challenge from Senator John Dingell asking for one more year to study this issue.

Walker Todd observed that combining the separation of securities powers from commercial banking and federal deposit insurance in the Glass-Steagall Act was controversial from the beginning. He argued that it would have been difficult at the time for the act's proponents to support the creation of deposit insurance while allowing banks to continue their affiliations with securities firms. He suggested that if Congress ever addresses Glass-Steagall in the future, it will have to do more on deposit insurance reform than was contained in FDICIA.

Todd also brought up a proposal (a bill introduced by Senator Nancy Kassebaum) that would allow well-capitalized banks willing to give up deposit insurance to engage in new activities. George Kaufman agreed that additional powers need to be tied in with deposit insurance reform, but he foresaw a problem arising when one of these large, uninsured banks has difficulties and turns to Congress. He believed that the only way to alleviate the problem of implicit insurance is with early intervention and resolution, so that banks know there are no exceptions. William Haraf noted that it would be more difficult for organizations with significant consumer banking activities to completely give up deposit insurance.

Haraf felt that another approach to Glass-Steagall reform was embodied in the Treasury proposal itself. This approach would separate securities activities from banking activities with a strong fire wall. Kaufman supported the subsidiary aspect of this strategy, but did not think setting up strong fire walls made sense, since one of the ideas behind allowing banks to engage in additional powers is the synergies that it creates. Kaufman also pointed to the securities industry as an example of a case where allowing institutions to engage in additional activities through subsidiaries works because there is a structured system of early intervention and resolution.

Glauber stressed that the industry needed to be resized and reshaped, but not *primarily* by enhancing bank powers. Instead, the most important vehicles were those of interstate branching and enforcement of higher capital standards.

Martin Mayer believed that market discipline on financial institutions could not be effective without improving bank accounting, especially the reporting of assets. Unfortunately, neither the government nor the private sector has faced up to this "intellectual weakness."

Dean Baker argued that before looking at expanding powers, one should concentrate on enhancing soundness regulation and ensure that banks will be closed down while they still have some capital. Establishing effective soundness regulation should occur before opening the floodgate by allowing interstate banking and by removing barriers to securities and other banking activities. Glauber disagreed with the notion that interstate banking would be inconsistent with safety and soundness. Instead he argued that it would allow banks to reduce risk through portfolio diversification.

Robert Litan highlighted the distinction between those scholars who focused on the microeconomic and those who focused on the macroeconomic aspects of bank regulation. The intellectual proponents of prompt corrective action essentially make their case on microeconomic grounds—namely, that curing the perverse incentives created by deposit insurance will prevent a misallocation of resources. However, recent critics of higher capital standards and prompt corrective action argue that any microbenefits of these policies can be more than offset by the macroeconomic costs due to an alleged excess of credit contraction. Litan noted that the intellectual groundwork for FDICIA was laid when the U.S. economy was booming, but when Congress enacted the bill the economy had entered a recession. Kaufman responded that macroelements did receive some attention before 1989, but many of these costs were viewed as transitory and thus passed over.

Discussion also touched on the topic of micromanagement. Glauber was troubled by the fact that standards existed for such things as the kinds of computers that banks have as part of the trip wires. Kaufman observed that these micromanagement standards were an attempt by the General Accounting Office to deal with the fact that book capital is considered a lagging indicator. If regulators were willing to go to market value accounting, then perhaps some of these micromanagement provisions would not be necessary.

With respect to higher capital standards themselves, Haraf agreed, in response to a question, that permitting banks to meet high capital ratios with subordinated debt would reduce the burden of a capital requirement significantly. But he noted that the use of subordinated debt is limited by international standards.

In considering how to prevent undercapitalized banks in particular from abusing deposit insurance, Kaufman said that with prompt closure or a higher closure level alone, the moral hazard problem will persist. He therefore supported the basic framework of FDICIA that combines prompt resolution with graduated penalties that become progressively stronger to mimic penalties that the market imposes on noninsured firms.

IMPLEMENTATION OF THE ACT: KEY REGULATIONS AND REGULATORY PROPOSALS

Edward Kane suggested that survey evidence showed that while some firms may have had difficulty obtaining bank credit, the problem was easing. In any event, monetary policymakers should have foreseen that higher bank capital standards would constrain lending and therefore should have pursued an easier monetary policy to compensate.

Kenneth Scott commented on the extent to which the regulatory implementation of FDICIA by the banking agencies thus far had furthered the congressional goals for its enactment. Under the section on prompt corrective action for capital deficiencies, the agencies have made no increase in required capital over the levels previously in effect; the promptness of their interventions remains to be demonstrated.

As for safety and soundness standards, the agencies have asked a series of questions, with draft language yet to come. However, they seem to be thinking more in terms of mandatory rules than in terms of standards for administrative action, an approach that will be very costly for bank operations if adhered to.

Scott noted that the act invited the agencies to alter their reporting requirements, disclosure rules, and accounting principles to reveal more about the actual economic worth of bank capital. The agencies, however, seem to have declined the invitation. Any improvement in the reliability of bank balance sheet numbers will have to come from the Financial Accounting Standards Board, which has been slowed by conflicting pressures from the SEC and the banking industry.

Karen Shaw found the trip wire section of the statute to be troublesome because of the difficulty of making minimum earnings and asset ratio numbers meaningful on a nationwide basis. What may work in one region may not work in another. Yet, if one sets more flexible standards, institutions will find it easier to follow a minimalist strategy.

Kane argued that the FDICIA standards should be treated as covenants. This would force regulators to leave a clear audit trail for the regulatory decisions made that effectively waive covenant rights.

Wendy Peter Abt looked at the relationship between credit availability and capital requirements. She disagreed with the notion that the risk weights in the Basle capital standards discourage banks from making loans. She observed that a middle market loan can be quite profitable and that it makes economic sense for banks to make loans as long as there are borrowers.

Lawrence Connell commented on the change in interest rate risk over the last ten years. He noted that the volatile part of interest rate risk today is due to uncertainties over prepayment rates on mortgaged-backed securities.

RESPONSES TO FDICIA: BANKS AND REGULATORS

Walker Todd applauded the provision in FDICIA that limits discount window assistance from the Federal Reserve when the capital adequacy level of the borrowing institution declines. But he also questioned the wisdom of another provision allowing the Federal Reserve to lend to an already insolvent bank when a systemic risk exception determination is made. Richard Carnell responded that the Federal Reserve insists that it is already adhering to the spirit of the new laws, although they have not taken effect, and that it does not want to lend to economically insolvent institutions. However, he said it will be difficult to know how much of this policy is being followed until two or three years in the future.

John Hawke believed that the purpose behind FDICIA's restriction of lending to insolvent or nearly insolvent banks was to address the "too big to fail" issue and to prevent the Federal Reserve from funding the runoff of uninsured deposits while the FDIC attempts to locate a buyer in an assisted transaction.

Martin Mayer commented that the problem with reported bank profit and capital figures was that both reflect the valuation of real estate. Looking at the current valuation of real estate, Mayer suspected that both the capital position and the income of banks are being greatly overstated by the willingness of regulators not to compel the writedown of assets.

Anthony Downs agreed that it is difficult to estimate real estate values and he added that they depend greatly on how one defines value. When there are very few buyers and many sellers then the prices reflect "liquidation value." Reevaluating bank assets at the liquidation value and as though they would all be sold the next day is not an accurate reflection of what those assets are really worth in the longer run. Many times the long-term value will be considerably higher than the liquidation value.

Richard Aspinwall addressed a question concerning the likelihood that banks will give up their charters. He suggested that shifts in costs relative to benefits are making this option increasingly appealing for a number of banks.

Philip Corwin argued that FDICIA shifted the paramount goal of financial regulation toward protecting the "bookkeeping fiction" known as the deposit insurance fund. The negative effects of regulatory micromanagement and reduced credit availability are a natural consequence of this fiction. Corwin added that the bankruptcy code made it easier for debtors to declare insolvency and avoid substantial repayment, further inducing lenders to be more reluctant to extend credit.

WHERE TO FROM HERE?

Many participants focused on the community development bank idea. Edward Ettin suggested that since community development banks are going to have risky portfolios, the amount of deposit insurance they receive should be limited.

Timmer disagreed with the assumption that lending in a poor area is riskier and has been more costly to the deposit insurance funds than lending to wealthy people. She argued that in fact the biggest losses to both banks and the deposit insurance funds were caused by large loans to large borrowers who ultimately defaulted. Litan observed that it nevertheless is more costly to lend in low-income areas in small amounts. In addition, he argued that the small amount of this lending so far indicates that bankers either do not know how to lend under these circumstances or they perceive such lending to be very risky.

Gillian Garcia pointed out that there are already credit unions out there, more than two hundred of which are involved in community development.

In response to a question about how banks would satisfy their Community Reinvestment Act obligations, Litan envisioned banks getting CRA credit by making an equity investment in a community development bank, where the investment must be more than a certain share of the investing bank's deposits or capital. He thought the banks making these equity contributions would want to have their representatives on the board of directors to monitor the community development banks. Litan also responded to the fears that some of these banks will fail. He pointed out that the social gains from aiding low-income areas with community development banks should far outweigh the costs imposed by the failures of some banks.

Paul Horvitz agreed that commercial banks would pay some money as a way of buying out of CRA. However, he questioned whether the best use for this money was to invest it in community development banks. Litan responded that these institutions can fill gaps in both mortgage lending, where there is a racial discrimination problem, as well as business lending, where there is a need for businesses in local communities but not enough capital.

On the broader issues affecting the banking industry as a whole, Bert Ely felt that the only deposit insurance crisis was that of the FSLIC. The bank insurance fund would have a positive balance of $9 to $10 billion at the end of 1992 based on actual closures. Ely suggested that the FDIC was encountering significant problems only with the savings banks it insures.

Ely also stated that insurance is a legitimate economic activity, but the federal deposit insurance system eliminated the possibility for banks to shift some portion of the risk of insolvency onto third parties. This created a less efficient intermediation system.

Finally, Ely noted the irony in the fact that because both FDICIA and FIRREA are driving intermediation out of the insured banking system, eventually the Federal Reserve will be in a crisis situation where it is forced to lend to a nonbanking institution. He concluded that taxpayer risk will not be eliminated by squeezing it out of the banking system but will only be shifted somewhere else.

Conference Participants
with their affiliations at the time of the conference

Wendy Peter Abt
Kellett Group

Jan Acton
Congressional Budget Office

William H. Adams
School of Law, George Mason University

Cheryl O. Alensio
Provident Bank of Maryland/Provident BankShares Corp.

Konrad S. Alt
Committee on Banking, Housing, and Urban Affairs, United States Senate

David J. Anderson
KeyCorp

Theresa Anderson
General Accounting Office

Linda M. Ashworth
Durell Journal of Money and Banking, Durell Institute

Ken Bacon
The Wall Street Journal

Dean Baker
Economic Policy Institute

James R. Barth
College of Business, Auburn University

Philip F. Bartholomew
Congressional Budget Office

Lawrence G. Baxter
Duke Law School

Richard "Sandy" Beach
Credit Union National Association, Inc.

Warren Belmar
Fulbright & Jaworski

Bradley D. Belt
Committee on Banking, Housing, and Urban Affairs, United States Senate

David W. Berson
Federal National Mortgage Association

Mike Bertelson
Beneficial Management

James C. Bothwell
General Accounting Office

Edward Bransilver
Shearman & Sterling

Peter E. Brereton
Society National Bank

William M. Brodhead
Plunkett & Cooney

Jeffrey Brown
Office of the Comptroller of the Currency

Jeremiah S. Buckley, Esq.
Thacher, Proffitt, & Wood

James M. Cain, Esq.
Sutherland, Asbill & Brennan

Paul Calem
Federal Reserve Bank of Philadelphia

Robert T. Clair
Federal Reserve Bank of Dallas

Anthony T. Cluff
Association of Reserve City Bankers

Michael E. Collins
Federal Reserve Bank of Philadelphia

Julie J. Coons
The Fuji Bank, Limited

Philip S. Corwin
American Bankers Association

Philippe Cottier
Embassy of Switzerland

Kevin D. Cramer
Jones, Day, Reavis & Pogue

Maureen Crowley
Federal Deposit Insurance Corporation

Jack Cushman
The New York Times

John Danforth
The Secura Group

Steve Davies
Bond Buyer

Smith W. Davis
Akin, Gump, Hauer, & Feld, LLP

Stella Dawson
Reuters

Frans de Neree tot Babberich
Royal Netherlands Embassy

Edward F. Dobbins
Mayer, Brown, & Platt

Theodore A. Doremus, Jr.
Davis, Polk, & Wardwell

Claudia Dziobek
Brookings Institution

Jennifer L. Eccles
Federal Deposit Insurance Corporation

Fritz Elmendorf
Consumer Bankers Association

Bert Ely
Ely & Company, Inc.

Catherine England
England Economics

Edward C. Ettin
Board of Governors of the Federal Reserve System

Frederick Evans
General Accounting Office

Martin T. Farmer
Barnett Banks, Inc.

Melanie L. Fein
Arnold & Porter

William Ferguson
Ferguson & Company

Jonathan L. Fiechter
Office of Thrift Supervision

Richard V. Fitzgerald
Muldoon, Murphy & Faucette

Dean Foust
Business Week Magazine

Annette Fribourg
Federal National Mortgage Association

Tim Friedman
Office of the Comptroller of the Currency

Michael Fuchs
Embassy of Denmark

Gillian G. Garcia
Committee on Banking, Housing, and Urban Affairs, United States Senate

R. Alton Gilbert
Federal Reserve Bank of St. Louis

Yvonne Gilmore, Esq.
National Association of Federal Credit Unions

Cynthia A. Glassman
Furash & Company

Dennis Glennon
Economic and Regulatory Policy Analysis, Economic and Policy Analysis, Office of the Comptroller of the Currency

Edward Golding
Freddie Mac

Susan K. Gordy
Susan K. Gordy Associates

James H. Gray, Jr.
Federal Housing Finance Board

Dave Hage
U.S. News & World Report

Howard O. Hagen
Dickinson/Throckmorton

Diana Hancock
Board of Governors of the Federal Reserve System

James Hearn
Congressional Budget Office

Robert Hetzel
Federal Reserve Bank of Richmond

Kelley Holland
Business Week

Stephen A. Hopkins
Citicorp/Citibank

David K. Horne
Federal Deposit Insurance Corporation

Paul Horvitz
Department of Finance, University of Houston

Susan Howard
The Jerome Levy Economics Institute of Bard College

Hunt Howell
Inter-American Development Bank

Laurie Itkin
National Conference of State Legislatures

David B. Jacobsohn
Hughes, Hubbard & Reed

David Jones
Board of Governors of the Federal Reserve System

Ike Jones
Resolution Trust Corporation

Kenneth D. Jones
General Accounting Office

Bill N. Kelly
Norwest Corporation

Joseph V. Kennedy
Budget Committee, U.S. House of Representatives

Douglas B. Kidd
Bankers Trust Company

Yoshihide Kimura
Japan Center for International Finance

Carl W. Klemme
National Westminster Bank

Jerry Knight
The Washington Post

Dennis R. Koons
NBD Bank, N.A.

Robert M. Krasne, Esq.
Williams & Connolly

Patrick J. Lawler
Committee on Banking, Housing, and Urban Affairs, United States Senate

J. Mark Leggett
NationsBank Corp.

Dennis J. Lehr
Hogan & Hartson

Martin Lowy
Martin Lowy & Associates

Thomas J. Lutton
Congressional Budget Office

Ezequiel L. Machado
Inter-American Development Bank

Yasuhiro Maehara
The Bank of Japan

Miles Maguire
American Banker Newsletters

James H. Mann
McDermott, Will & Emery

Katsumi Matsubara
Jiji Press, Japan

Barbara Matthews
Institute of International Finance

Martin Mayer
Independent journalist

Robert N. McCauley
Federal Reserve Bank of New York

Michael McCullough
Davis, Polk, & Wardwell

Susan McInerney
Bureau of National Affairs, Inc.

Mike McNamee
Business Week

Timothy R. McTaggert
Committee on Banking, Housing, and Urban Affairs, United States Senate

Kathleen P. McTighe
New York Bankers Association

Loretta J. Mester
Finance Department, The Wharton School

Thomas Miller
Competitive Enterprise Institute

John Mingo
Board of Governors of the Federal Reserve System

Hyman P. Minsky
The Jerome Levy Economics Institute of Bard College

Sanjay Mongia
The Jerome Levy Economics Institute of Bard College

Larry R. Mote
Federal Reserve Bank of Chicago

C. Westbrook Murphy
Price Waterhouse

Jeanne-Marie Murphy
Credit Union National Association

Arthur Murton
Federal Deposit Insurance Corporation

Raymond Natter
Committee on Banking, Housing, and Urban Affairs, United States Senate

Marlene N. Nicholson
Barclays Bank PLC

Brian Olasov
Long, Aldridge & Norman

Franz M. Oppenheimer, Esq.
Fort & Schlefer

Dimitri B. Papadimitriou
The Jerome Levy Economics Institute of Bard College

Joseph K. Pascale
Institute for Strategy Development

Wayne Passmore
Board of Governors of the Federal Reserve System

Robert E. Patterson
Pennsylvania Blue Shield

Ira Paull
Committee on Banking, Housing, and Urban Affairs, United States Senate

Neal Peterson
Congressman Bruce F. Vento

Ronnie J. Phillips
The Jerome Levy Economics Institute of Bard College

Alfred M. Pollard
Savings & Community Bankers of America

Elizabeth E. Racer
Durell Institute

John C. Rasmus
American Bankers Association

F. Stevens Redburn
U.S. Office of Management and Budget

Barb Rehm
American Banker

Alan Rhinesmith
U.S. Office of Management and Budget

Alan Rice
Pratt's Letter

Robert A. Richard
Conference on State Bank Supervisors

Ken Robinson
Federal Reserve Bank of Dallas

Justine Rodriguez
U.S. Office of Management and Budget

Frank M. Salinger
ADVANTA Corporation

David Sands
The Washington Times

Kevan Sandy
Bureau of National Affairs, Inc.

William H. Satchell, Esq.
O'Melveny & Myers

Elliot Schwartz
Congressional Budget Office

Robert Schweitzer
Department of Finance, University of Delaware

Robin S. Seiler
Congressional Budget Office

Gordon H. Sellon, Jr.
Federal Reserve Bank of Kansas City

Krysten Senci
Japan Center for International Finance

J. Michael Shepherd
Sullivan & Cromwell

James Smalhout
Brookings Institution

Daniel C. Smith
Federal National Mortgage Association

Kenneth Spong
Federal Reserve Bank of Kansas City

David Stahl
Savings & Community Bankers of America

Susan Stawick
Future's World News

Nancy Marie Stiles
Silver, Freedman & Taff

Stephan Swain
General Accounting Office

Peter Swire
School of Law, University of Virginia

Peter Szekeley
Reuters

Charles Szlenker
Federal Housing Finance Board

Brent T. Thompson
National Association of Manufacturers

Elizabeth Tibbals
New York State Banking Department

Walker F. Todd
Federal Reserve Bank of Cleveland

Robert Van Order
Freddie Mac

Stephen J. Verdier
Independent Bankers Association of America

John Vialet
General Accounting Office

David A. Walker
School of Business, Georgetown University

John R. Walter
Federal Reserve Bank of Richmond

Ronald D. Watson
Custodial Trust Company

William R. Watson
Federal Deposit Insurance Corporation

Margery Waxman
Sidley and Austin

Harris Weinstein, Esq.
Office of Thrift Supervision

Monica Welch
EDS

Brad G. Welling
American International Group

Gary M. Welsh, Esq.
Prather, Seeger, Doolittle & Farmer

Marilyn Werber
Congress Daily

Jeffrey Winograd
Winograd Group

Craig G. Wolfson
Wells Fargo Bank

Patrick Woodall
Public Citizen

Michael Young
Farm Credit Administration